A Guide to the Civil War in Georgia

Robert C. Jones

Robert C. Jones
POB 1775
Kennesaw, GA 30156

jone442@bellsouth.net
rcjbooks.com

"A Guide to the Civil War in Georgia", Copyright 2013 by Robert C. Jones. All rights reserved.

First Edition

ISBN: 149371497X
EAN-13: 978-1493714971

Contents

- Contents...3
- Introduction...5
- Leaders...6
  - Robert Toombs..6
  - Alexander Stephens..11
  - Howell Cobb...16
  - Major General Joseph Wheeler, CSA................23
  - William Joseph Hardee....................................28
  - Governor Joseph E. Brown..............................32
  - Major General William Henry Talbot Walker....34
- Battles, Raids and Campaigns.................................39
  - Great Locomotive Chase.................................39
  - Chickamauga...45
  - Ringgold Gap...53
  - Sherman's Atlanta Campaign..........................54
  - Stoneman's Raid...71
  - Sherman's March to the Sea..........................75
  - Allatoona Pass..86
- Training Camps...91
  - Camp McDonald/Phillips Legion.....................92
  - Camp Stephens..93
- Forts..96
- Manufacturing..105
- Hospitals..113
- Headquarters..124
- Prison Camps..132
  - Andersonville...132
  - Millen...137
- Railroads...140
  - Western & Atlantic (Chattanooga)..............140
  - Georgia Railroad (Augusta, Charleston, Richmond)....143
  - Macon & Western (Macon, Savannah)........147
  - Atlanta & West Point (Montgomery)..........149

Central Railroad..150
Cemeteries...157
Sources..168
Appendix One – Battles in Georgia....................................171
Appendix Two - General Officers Of The Confederate Army Appointed From Georgia..178
Appendix Three - Local Designations of Georgia Troops in the Confederate Army...181
The Author on YouTube..204
About the Author..205

Introduction

Georgia has a rich Civil War heritage, perhaps second only to Virginia. Several major battles were fought here – Chickamauga, Kennesaw Mountain, Battle of Atlanta, Peachtree Creek – and two major campaigns that pretty much destroyed the Confederacy – Sherman's Atlanta Campaign, and Sherman's March to the Sea. Two significant prisoner of war camps were located in Georgia – Andersonville, and Millen (Camp Lawton).

This book will examine the Civil War in Georgia, with special emphasis on what is left today. Battlefields, hospitals, headquarters, training camps, manufacturing sites, and National and Confederate Cemeteries dot the landscape throughout northwestern and central Georgia. Addresses for many of the sites are included for mobile GPS units.

Three appendixes contain information pulled either directly or indirectly from a 1909 book *Georgia in the War, 1861-1865*, by Charles Edgeworth Jones. The appendixes contain information on battles in Georgia, generals from Georgia, and the local names of all Georgia units ("Spalding Greys", etc.), and their associated official designation.

I hope you enjoy this look at the Civil War in Georgia.

Robert C. Jones
Kennesaw, GA
November 2013

Leaders

Robert Toombs

Date	Events
July 2, 1810	Born near Washington, Georgia
1828	Graduates from Union College, in Schenectady, New York
1829/30	Studies law at University of Virginia Law School in Charlottesville, Virginia
March 18, 1830	Admitted to Georgia bar
November 1830	Marries Julia A. Dubose
1836	Commands a company in the Creek War
1838	Elected to Georgia House of Representatives
1844/53	Elected to United States House of Representatives from Georgia
March 4, 1853 – February 4, 1861	U.S. Senator from Georgia
June 24, 1856	Proposes Toombs Bill, which proposes a constitutional convention in Kansas to determine slavery issues
December 22, 1860	Publicly calls for secession of Georgia by March 4, 1861
January 7, 1861	Farewell address to U.S. Senate
January 16, 1861	Member of the state sovereignty convention in Milledgeville, Georgia; votes for secession
February 25, 1861 – July 25, 1861	Confederate Secretary of State
July 19, 1861	Brigadier general in the Army of the Potomac

Date	Events
September 15, 1862	Defends Burnside Bridge for several hours at the Battle of Antietam with 400 Georgia sharpshooters
March 3, 1863	Resigns his commission in the Confederate Army to become a colonel in the Georgia Militia (later promoted to brigadier general)
December, 1864	Helps defend Savannah during Sherman's March to the Sea
May 14, 1865	Federals soldiers appear at his home to arrest him as a key instigator of the rebellion (along with Jefferson Davis, John Slidell, Alexander Stephens and Howell Cobb; Toombs flees to Cuba and then Europe
1867	Returns to Georgia, but refuses to take the oath of loyalty
1877	A major architect of the Georgia Constitution
December 15, 1885	Dies in Washington, Georgia

Robert Toombs had a varying political and military resume, serving as a Georgia Congressman, U.S. Congressman, U.S. Senator, Confederate Secretary of State and a Brigadier General in both the Confederate Army and the Georgia Militia. He only served 6 months in his post as Confederate Secretary of State, as he and Jefferson Davis did not get along. Toombs probably felt that he, and not Davis, should have been made President of the Confederacy.

While the military career of Toombs was not lengthy or especially distinguished, he does hold one great distinction as a Brigadier General. It was Toombs and 400 sharpshooters that held what is now known as the Burnside Bridge at Antietam for several hours, when a whole Union Corps made repeated attempts to cross it. Toombs was wounded enough in the fighting that he was sent home to recuperate. It should also be pointed out that Toombs helped defend Georgia against Sherman in both the Atlanta Campaign, and, more prominently, during the March to the Sea.

Robert Toombs[1]

As a politician, Toombs helped lead Georgia to secede from the Union in 1861. On December 7, 1860, Toombs gave a fiery speech before the Georgia legislature advocating secession. Some excerpts follow.

> Gentlemen Of The General Assembly—I very much regret, in appearing before you at your request, to address you on the present state of the country, and the prospect before us, that I can bring you no good tidings. The stern, steady march of events

---

[1] Library of Congress http://www.loc.gov/pictures/item/brh2003000349/PP/

has brought us in conflict with our non-Slaveholding confederates upon the fundamental principles of our compact of Union. We have not sought this conflict; we have sought too long to avoid it; our forbearance has been construed into weakness, our magnanimity into fear, until the vindication of our manhood, as well as the defence of our rights, is required at our hands. The door of conciliation and compromise is finally closed by our adversaries, and it remains only to us to meet the conflict with the dignity and firmness of men worthy of freedom...

Let us examine what they [the North] are at as private citizens. By the law of nations, founded on natural justice, no nation nor the subjects or citizens of any nation, have the right to disturb the peace or security of any other nation of people, much less to conspire, excite insurrection, discontent or the commission of crimes among them, and all these are held to be good causes of war. For twenty years this party has, by abolition societies, by publications made by them, by the public press,, through the pulpit and their own legislative halls, and every effort—by reproaches, by abuse, by vilification, by slander—to disturb our security, our tranquility—to excite discontent between the different classes of our people, and to excite our slaves to insurrection. No nation in the world would submit to such conduct from any other nation. I will not willingly do so from this abolition party. I demand the protection of my State government, to whom I owe my allegiance. I wish it distinctly understood that it is the price of my allegiance. You are here, constitutional legislators—I make the demand today of yon. Gentlemen, I have thus shown you the violations of our constitutional rights by our confederates; I have shown you that they are plain, palpable, deliberate and dangerous; that they are committed by the executive, legislative and judicial departments of the State governments of our confederates—that all their wrongs are approved by the people of these States, I say the time has come to redress these acknowledged wrongs, and to avert even greater evils of which these are but the signs and symbols. But I am asked, why do you demand action now? The question is both appropriate and important— ought to be frankly met. The abolitionists say yon are raising clamor because you were beaten in the election. The falsity of this statement needs no confirmation. Look to our past history for its refutation. Some excellent citizens and able men in Georgia say the election of any man constitutionally is no cause for a dissolution of the Union;

that position is calculated only to mislead, and not to enlighten. It is not the issue. I say the election of Lincoln, with all of its surroundings, is sufficient. What is the significance of his election? It is the endorsement by the non-slaveholding States of all those acts of aggression upon our rights by all these States, Legislatures, Governors, Judges and people. He is elected by the perpetrators of these wrongs with the purpose and intent to aid and support them in wrong-doing...

We are said to be a happy and prosperous people. We have been, because we have hitherto maintained our ancient rights and liberties—we will be until we surrender them. They are in danger; come, freemen, to the rescue...Withdraw yourselves from such a confederacy [the United States]; it is your right to do so; your duty to do so. I know not why the abolitionists should object to it, unless they want you to torture and plunder you. If they resist this great sovereign right, make another war of independence, for that then will be the question; fight its battles over again; reconquer liberty and independence. As for me, I will take any place in the great conflict for rights which you may assign. I will take none in the Federal Government during Mr. Lincoln's administration.

If you desire a Senator after the 4th of March you must elect one in my place. I have served you in the State and national counsels for nearly a quarter of a century, without once losing your confidence. I am yet ready for the public service when honor and duty call. I will serve you anywhere where it will not degrade and dishonor my country. Make my name infamous, forever, if you will, but save Georgia. I have pointed out your wrongs, your danger, your duty. You have claimed nothing but that rights be respected, and that justice be done. Emblazon it on your banner, fight for it, win it, or perish in the effort. (Speech of Hon. Robert Toombs, *The Crisis*. Delivered Before the Georgia Legislature, December 7, 1860)

Toombs is sometimes referred to as the "Last Rebel", because he never took the oath to return to the Union, not did he ask for a pardon from the Congress (Toombs was on a small list of "key instigators" of the rebellion). Because he was an unrepentant rebel, he couldn't vote or run for political office, but he had a successful law practice after the War, and was a leading force in the creation of the post-Reconstruction Georgia Constitution of 1877.

Alexander Stephens

Date	Events
February 11, 1812	Born in Taliaferro County, Georgia
1832	Graduates from Franklin College (now University of Georgia)
1834	Passes bar, and practices law in Crawfordville, Georgia
1842	Elected to Georgia Senate
October 2, 1843 – March 3, 1859	U.S. Congressman from Georgia
1845	Supports annexation of Texas
1846	Disapproves of the Mexican War
September 3, 1848	The frail Stephens is stabbed repeatedly by Judge Francis Cone, after an argument over the Mexican War
1848	Campaigns for Zachary Taylor for president
June 7, 1853	In a train wreck near Macon
November 14, 1860	Urges preservation of the Union in Milledgeville
January 16, 1861	Votes against secession in the Georgia secession convention
February 11, 1861 – May 11, 1865	Vice-President of the Confederate States of America
March 21, 1861	Supports slavery in his *Cornerstone Speech* in Savannah, Georgia
1861	Advises against firing on Fort Sumter
mid-1863	Davis sends him on a mission to Washington to reopen prisoner exchanges; Lincoln refuses to see

Date	Events
	him
March 16, 1864	Makes a speech criticizing Davis for supporting a draft, and for suspending *habeas corpus*
February 3, 1865	Meeting with Lincoln off the coast of Virginia in the Hampton Roads Conference
May 11, 1865	Arrested in Crawfordville, Georgia and imprisoned in Fort Warren, Boston Harbor
1866	Elected to U.S. Senate from Georgia, but is kept from taking his seat by Reconstruction limitations
1867/70	Author of *A Constitutional View of the Late War Between the States* (2 volumes)
1871, 1883	Author of *History of the United States*
December 1, 1873 – November 4, 1882	U.S. Congressman from Georgia
November 4, 1882 – March 4, 1883	Governor of Georgia
March 4, 1883	Dies in Atlanta, Georgia
August 18, 1905	Stephens County, Georgia created

Alexander Stephens was a successful lawyer and politician. Before the War, he served in the Georgia Senate (finishing out the term of Mark Anthony Cooper), and then served as a long-time Congressman from Georgia. After the War, he was elected to the U.S. Senate in 1866, but was barred from serving. He eventually served as both a U.S. Congressman, and finally, Governor of Georgia. Stephens served as the first – and only – Vice-president of the Confederate States of America.

Stephens was not an unqualified proponent of secession. As late as 1860 and 1861, he made speeches recommending against secession, and voted against Georgia seceding at the Georgia secession convention. Once secession was a reality, he recommended against firing on Fort Sumter. However, once the War started, his actions and speeches as Vice-President were strongly pro-slavery and pro-Confederacy.

In his *Cornerstone* speech of March 21, 1861, Stephens stated that the cornerstone of the new (Confederate) government rested on the "great truth that the negro is not equal to the white man". He also discussed reasons why the Confederacy would be successful as an independent nation. Some excerpts follow.

> Our new government is founded upon exactly the opposite idea; its foundations are laid, its cornerstone rests, upon the great truth that the negro is not equal to the white man; that slavery subordination to the superior race is his natural and normal condition. This, our new government, is the first, in the history of the world, based upon this great physical, philosophical, and moral truth. This truth has been slow in the process of its development, like all other truths in the various departments of science. It has been so even amongst us. Many who hear me, perhaps, can recollect well, that this truth was not generally admitted, even within their day. The errors of the past generation still clung to many as late as twenty years ago. Those at the North, who still cling to these errors, with a zeal above knowledge, we justly denominate fanatics. All fanaticism springs from an aberration of the mind from a defect in reasoning. It is a species of insanity. One of the most striking characteristics of insanity, in many instances, is forming correct conclusions from fancied or erroneous premises; so with the anti-slavery fanatics. Their conclusions are right if their premises were. They assume that the negro is equal, and hence conclude that he is entitled to equal privileges and rights with the white man. If their premises were correct, their conclusions would be logical and just but their premise being wrong, their whole argument fails. I recollect once of having heard a gentleman from one of the northern States, of great power and ability, announce in the House of Representatives, with imposing effect, that we of the South would be compelled, ultimately, to yield upon this subject of slavery,

that it was as impossible to war successfully against a principle in politics, as it was in physics or mechanics. That the principle would ultimately prevail. That we, in maintaining slavery as it exists with us, were warring against a principle, a principle founded in nature, the principle of the equality of men. The reply I made to him was, that upon his own grounds, we should, ultimately, succeed, and that he and his associates, in this crusade against our institutions, would ultimately fail. The truth announced, that it was as impossible to war successfully against a principle in politics as it was in physics and mechanics, I admitted; but told him that it was he, and those acting with him, who were warring against a principle. They were attempting to make things equal which the Creator had made unequal...

The idea has been given out at the North, and even in the border States, that we are too small and too weak to maintain a separate nationality. This is a great mistake. In extent of territory we embrace five hundred and sixty-four thousand square miles and upward. This is upward of two hundred thousand square miles more than was included within the limits of the original thirteen States. It is an area of country more than double the territory of France or the Austrian empire. France, in round numbers, has but two hundred and twelve thousand square miles. Austria, in round numbers, has two hundred and forty-eight thousand square miles. Ours is greater than both combined. It is greater than all France, Spain, Portugal, and Great Britain, including England, Ireland, and Scotland, together. In population we have upward of five millions, according to the census of 1860; this includes white and black. The entire population, including white and black, of the original thirteen States, was less than four millions in 1790, and still less in 76, when the independence of our fathers was achieved. If they, with a less population, dared maintain their independence against the greatest power on earth, shall we have any apprehension of maintaining ours now?

In point of material wealth and resources, we are greatly in advance of them. The taxable property of the Confederate States cannot be less than twenty-two hundred millions of dollars! This, I think I venture but little in saying, may be considered as five times more than the colonies possessed at the time they achieved their independence. Georgia, alone, possessed last year, according to the report of our comptroller-general, six hundred and seventy-two millions of taxable property...With such an area of territory as we have-with such an amount of population-with a climate and soil unsurpassed by any on the face of the earth-with such resources already at our command-with productions which control the commerce of the world-who can entertain any apprehensions as to our ability to succeed, whether others join us or not?[2] (Cornerstone speech, March 21, 1861, Savannah, Georgia)

Alexander Stephens[3]

Jefferson Davis and Stephens were not elected as a ticket. As a matter of fact, Stephens was inaugurated several days before Davis. They were not natural political allies, and Stephens often spoke out against policies of Davis (suspending *habeas corpus*, conscription).

---
[2] http://teachingamericanhistory.org/library/index.asp?documentprint=76
[3] Library of Congress http://www.loc.gov/pictures/item/cwp2003001868/PP/

On February 3, 1865, on a ship near near Fort Monroe in Newport News, Virginia, Stephens met with Abraham Lincoln and Secretary of State William H. Seward in an attempt to negotiate a peace treaty. Nothing came of the conference, and the War continued for another several months.

Alexander Stephens, although reluctant to support secession, became the one and only Vice-President of the Confederacy.

Howell Cobb

Date	Events
September 7, 1815	Born in Jefferson County, Georgia
1834	Graduates from the University of Georgia
May 26, 1835	Marries Mary Ann Lamar
1836	Admitted to bar
1837	Appointed by the Georgia state legislature to be solicitor general for the Western Judicial Circuit of Georgia
March 4, 1843 – March 4, 1851	Congressman from Georgia, United States House of Representatives
December 22, 1849 – March 4, 1851	Speaker of the House of Representatives, United States; in 1850, he was next in line for the presidency when Zachary Taylor died, but could not serve because he was not yet 35
November 5, 1851 – November 9, 1853	Governor of Georgia
1856	Publishes *A Scriptural Examination of the Institution of Slavery*
March 7, 1857	Secretary of the Treasury, United States (under

Date	Events
– December 8, 1860	James Buchanan)
1857	Financial Panic
February 24, 1861	Influential member of the secession convention in Montgomery, Alabama
February 4, 1861 – February 17, 1862	Speaker of the Provisional Confederate Congress
February 4, 1861 - February 18, 1861	Provisional Head of State, Confederate States of America
February 13, 1862	Becomes a brigadier general in the Army of Northern Virginia
Spring 1862	Involved in negotiations with the Union regarding prisoner exchanges
September 9, 1863	Promoted to Major General, and placed in command of the District of Georgia and Florida; recommends building what would become Andersonville prison
1864	Commands Georgia reserve corps during Sherman's Atlanta Campaign and the March to the Sea; Sherman leveled Cobb's plantation during the latter campaign (November 22, 1864)
April 16, 1865	Leads Confederate forces in the Battle of Columbus, Georgia, the official closing battle of the Civil War
April 20, 1865	Surrenders in Macon, Georgia
1868	Receives a presidential pardon; speaks out against Radical Republicans and Radical Reconstruction
October 9, 1868	Dies in New York City, New York of a heart attack; his body is interred at the Oconee Hill Cemetery in Athens, Georgia

Howell Cobb, a Georgia boy through and through, was a lawyer, politician, Civil War general and author. As a politician, he served multiple terms in the U.S. Congress, and was Speaker of the House for two years. He also served a term as Governor of Georgia, and served as Secretary of the Treasury of the United States under James Buchanan. For a year (1861/62), he served as Speaker of the Provisional Confederate Congress. During that period, he was briefly the highest ranking official in the Confederacy (before Davis and Stephens were sworn into office).

"The Southern Confederacy - Senate Chamber in the Capitol at Montgomery, Alabama, during open session - the Hon. Howell Cobb presiding"[4]

Cobb was a political ally of Alexander Stephens and Robert Toombs. He strongly supported the institution of slavery, and supported its expansion into the territories. He was not a "Fire-Eater", though, like William Yancey — Cobb didn't support secession until it became clear that that was the direction that the Southern states were going.

---

[4] Library of Congress http://www.loc.gov/pictures/item/99614054/

Major General Howell Cobb[5]

As a general, Major General Howell Cobb served first in the Army of Northern Virginia. He fought in the Peninsula Campaign and at Antietam. In 1863, he was put in charge of the District of Georgia and Florida, and eventually was in charge of all Georgia reservists. He was one of several generals[6] trying to formulate a defensive strategy for central Georgia during Sherman's March to the Sea.

During the March to the Sea, Sherman specially targeted the house and plantation of Howell Cobb. From Sherman's *Memoirs*:

> So I started on foot, and found on the main road a good double-hewed-log house, in one room of which Colonel Poe, Dr. Moore,

---

[5] Library of Congress http://www.loc.gov/pictures/item/2006687471/
[6] Others included Gustavus Smith, William Hardee, Pierre Beauregard, Robert Toombs

and others, had started a fire. I sent back orders to the "plum-bushes" to bring our horses and saddles up to this house, and an orderly to conduct our headquarter wagons to the same place. In looking around the room, I saw a small box, like a candle-box, marked "Howell Cobb," and, on inquiring of a negro, found that we were at the plantation of General Howell Cobb, of Georgia, one of the leading rebels of the South, then a general in the Southern army, and who had been Secretary of the United States Treasury in Mr. Buchanan's time. Of course, we confiscated his property, and found it rich in corn, beans, peanuts, and sorghum-molasses. Extensive fields were all round the house; **I sent word back to General Davis to explain whose plantation it was, and instructed him to spare nothing. That night huge bonfires consumed the fence-rails, kept our soldiers warm, and the teamsters and men, as well as the slaves, carried off an immense quantity of corn and provisions of all sorts.** (*Memoirs of General William T. Sherman*, by William Tecumseh Sherman; emphasis added)[7]

Like William Yancey or George Fitzhugh, Cobb was fully supportive of the institution of slavery. Cobb wrote a book of some prominence in the years before the War entitled *A Scriptural examination of the institution of slavery in the United States*. It is perhaps the best example of the Southern view in the mid-1800s that slavery was both of "divine appointment", and fully in line with Biblical tenets.

From the *Preface*:

> It must not be supposed, that in the performance of this task we desire to present an apology for slavery, or to conciliate favor for it; we have no such intention or object in view. An institution of Divine appointment does not need the aid of human writers, further than an explanation of its meaning.
>
> Why should any one be astonished at slavery? This is not the only time that it has been employed as a means of working out great purposes. God's chosen and peculiar people; they who first

---

[7] http://www.sonofthesouth.net/union-generals/sherman/memoirs/general-sherman-march-sea.htm

composed the Church; they to whom the oracles of salvation were delivered; they of whom the prophets were; they from whom the Redeemer of the world sprang, were enslaved in as hard, perhaps in much harder bondage, than has ever been experienced by Africans in the United States—a bondage from which they were delivered only after a series of the most astonishing displays of the Divine displeasure, inflicted upon their oppressors for their obstinacy in refusing "to let the people go."

Nor was Egyptian bondage the only bondage they experienced, for their history shows that there were repeated instances of captivity, during which they were subject to the most degrading and humiliating slavery. And their history further shows, that these instances of captivity were inflicted as punishments upon them for their unfaithfulness to God, in disobeying His commands. Nor was this mode of punishment confined to the Hebrews; for, the sacred record shows, that it was frequently threatened and inflicted upon other nations. Indeed, we may say, slavery has ever been a common mode of divine punishment inflicted upon nations.

From a section entitled "Regulation of Slavery":

Slavery in the Church, contemporaneous with its organization.— The Bible teaches that Abraham and his household were the first members of the Church of God, under its present organization. There can be nothing, therefore, more interesting than to inquire who composed that household. The Bible says, "And Abraham took Sarai his wife, and Lot his brother's son, and all their substance that they had gathered, and the souls they had gotten in Haran: and they went forth to go into the land of Canaan, and into the land of Canaan they came."

That the words, "and the souls they had gotten in Haran," mean slaves, no one can for a moment doubt. Both Jewish and Christian commentators agree in this explanation. Jenks, in the Comprehensive Commentary, says, "They took with them the souls they had gotten; that is, the servants they had bought; part of their substance, but called souls to remind masters that their servants have souls, precious souls, which they ought to take care of and provide for." This must be regarded as the natural and correct import of the words under consideration; they are incapable of sustaining any other interpretation. That this view is correct, will be seen by its conformity to other instructions given to Abraham.

Circumcision.—Circumcision was an ordinance which God established in the Church at the time of its organization: "And God said unto Abraham, Thou shalt keep my covenant therefore; thou, and thy seed after thee, in their generations. This is my covenant which ye shall keep between me and you, and thy seed after thee; Every man-child among you shall be circumcised. And ye shall circumcise the flesh of your foreskin; and it shall be a token of the covenant betwixt me and you."

Subjects of Circumcision.—"And he that is eight days old, shall be circumcised among you; every man-child in your generations; he that is born in thy house, or bought with money of any stranger, which is not of thy seed. He that is born in thy house, and he that is bought with thy money, must needs be circumcised: and my covenant shall be in your flesh, for an everlasting covenant."

Commands so explicit could not be misunderstood; they were faithfully obeyed. Abraham is to be regarded as standing in the midst of a sinful world, "The friend of God." There is much in this divine arrangement to call forth our gratitude and thankfulness—more particularly that provision which is made for slaves becoming partakers of the faith of Abraham, or in the covenant made with him. The duty is here imposed upon the parent of consecrating his infant child to God, and upon the master of, in like manner, consecrating his infant slave. The duty imposed allows of no difference between the parent and the master; both are under the same obligation. This arrangement has no respect to condition, and contemplates the dedication of all children to God; for all children should be reared in the Church.

In obedience to the command, "Abraham took Ishmael his son, and all that were born in his house, and that were bought with his money; every male among the men of Abraham's house, and circumcised the flesh of their foreskin, in the self-same day, as God had said unto him.

"And Abraham was ninety years old and nine, when he was circumcised in the flesh of his foreskin. And Ishmael his son, was thirteen years old, when he was circumcised in the flesh of his foreskin. "And all the men of his house, born in the house, and bought with money of the stranger, were circumcised with him."

Major General Joseph Wheeler, CSA

Major General Joseph Wheeler (1836-1906)[8]

Date	Events
September 10, 1836	Born in Augusta, Georgia
July 1, 1859	Graduates from West Point, 19th out of 22 in his class
June 26, 1860	Serves in the Regiment of Mounted Rifles in the New Mexico Territory
September 1, 1860	Promoted to the rank of second lieutenant

---

[8] Library of Congress http://www.loc.gov/pictures/item/cwp2003000446/PP/

Date	Events
March 16, 1861	Joins the Confederate Army as a first lieutenant serving in the Georgia state militia artillery
September 4, 1861	Promoted to colonel of the 19th Alabama Infantry Regiment
April 1862	Serves under Braxton Bragg at the Battle of Shiloh
September/ October 1862	Given command of the 2nd Cavalry Brigade of the Left Wing in the Army of Mississippi
October 30, 1862	Promoted to brigadier general after fighting at Perryville
November 27, 1862	Injured at La Vergne, Tennessee from an artillery shell
December 1862	Successful cavalry raid against the Army of the Cumberland during their advance from Nashville
1863	Writes *A Revised System of Cavalry Tactics, for the Use of the Cavalry and Mounted Infantry, C.S.A*
January 12/13, 1863	Effective cavalry raid against Union forces in Tennessee at Harpeth Shoals
January 20, 1863	Upon Bragg's recommendation, promoted to major general
May 1, 1863	Receives Thanks of the Confederate Congress for his action at Harpeth Shoals
September 1863	Wheeler is criticized for not letting Braxton Bragg know the location of Rosecrans' army in the month leading up to the Battle of Chickamauga
September 19/20, 1863	Cavalry commander at the Battle of Chickamauga
October 2, 1863	Successful cavalry raid at Anderson's Cross Roads in central Tennessee
November 25/27, 1863	Covers Bragg's retreat into North Georgia after the Battle of Missionary Ridge
July 30, 1864	Routs Edward McCook's cavalry at the Battle of Brown's Mill
August 14/15, 1864	Cavalry Raid on Dalton, Georgia tears up some W&A track, but the Union garrison there doesn't

Date	Events
	surrender
Late August, 1864	Raiding in Tennessee, Wheeler's cavalry is not present during the final days of Hood's defense of Atlanta
November/December 1864	Wheeler is the only effective fighting force against Sherman during the latter's March to the Sea
February 11, 1865	Defeats Union Brigadier-General Judson Kilpatrick at Aiken, South Carolina, but is soon relieved of his command of the Confederate cavalry, and placed under the command of Wade Hampton
March 19/20, 1865	Fights under Hampton at the Battle of Bentonville, North Carolina
May 1865	Wheeler is captured by Union troops in Conyer's Station, Georgia, and imprisoned in Fort Monroe
June 8, 1865	Wheeler is paroled, and released from confinement
1882	Wins special election to the U.S. Congress
1883	Authors *Fitz-John Porter*
1884/1900	U.S. Congressman
1898	• Appointed major general of volunteers by U.S. President William McKinley, to head cavalry forces in Cuba • Appears in silent film *Surrender of General Toral* (with William Rufus Shafter)
June 24, 1898	Battle of Las Guasimas, Cuba (near Santiago)
July 1, 1898	Battle of San Juan Hill. Theodore Roosevelt and the Rough Riders serve under Wheeler.
1899	• Authors *Confederate Military History: Alabama* • Authors *The Santiago Campaign*
August 1899	Commands First Brigade, Second Division in the Philippine-American War
June 16, 1900	Commissioned as brigadier general in the regular army
January 25, 1906	Dies in New York, New York, and is buried in Arlington Cemetery

Date	Events
November 5, 1912	Wheeler County, Georgia is established (located SE of Macon)
July 18, 1917	Camp Wheeler, Macon, is established (decommissioned January 19, 1946)
1936	Wheeler Lake and Wheeler Dam in Alabama open
1938	Wheeler National Wildlife Refuge near Decatur, Alabama opens
1965	Joseph Wheeler High School in Marietta, Georgia opens
1997	Portrayed by Gary Busey in the miniseries *Rough Riders*

Joseph Wheeler was, along with Nathan Bedford Forrest, the most significant Confederate cavalry officer in the West during the Civil War. Wheeler fought in a number of battles and raids throughout the War, including Shiloh, the Chickamauga Campaign, the Tullahoma Campaign, the Chattanooga Campaign, the Knoxville Campaign, Sherman's Atlanta Campaign and March to the Sea, and the Carolinas Campaign. He was a key player in the defeat of the Stoneman/McCook Raid into central Georgia in July of 1864.

Wheeler was the sole Confederate (as opposed to Militia) fighting force that challenged Sherman during the March to the Sea. Most of his battles with Sherman were with his opposing number, Judson Kilpatrick, but a couple of times he had Union infantry arrayed against him (Griswoldville, Waynesboro). He successfully helped defend Macon against a cavalry raid by Kilpatrick in the early days of the March.

There was some controversy regarding Wheeler's performance during the War. He was criticized for not letting Braxton Bragg know the location of Rosecrans' army in the month leading up to the Battle of Chickamauga. He was relieved of his position as head of the Cavalry for the Army of Tennessee during Sherman's Carolinas Campaign, because a review by a staff officer named Colonel Roman on Beauregard's staff had criticized the lax discipline in Wheeler's corps. Interestingly, the officers of "Camp Humes's Cavalry Division, In The Field, Wayne County, N. C., April 3d, 1865." wrote a document in strong support of their longtime leader, Joseph Wheeler:

> Resolved 1st, That since the organization of this cavalry corps we have followed General Wheeler, and have always found him vigilant, active and brave, and that during this long period, now over eighteen months, he has never been absent from his post for an hour, constantly giving his personal attention to the interests of the cause. He has been foremost in fight, in most instances even leading and directing the movements of the skirmish line. In every exigency his presence inspiring the utmost confidence on the part of all his troops...
>
> ...Resolved 4th, That, while we would not underrate the distinguished services rendered or detract from the merited laurels won by General Hampton, we desire to say in most unmistakable terms that we entertain now, as we have always done, the most unbounded confidence in General Wheeler as a man and as an officer, and where he leads we will cheerfully follow.[9]

Wheeler served as a major general of volunteers in the Spanish American War, and had Theodore Roosevelt's Rough Riders under his command.

---

[9] *Campaigns of Wheeler and His Cavalry, 1862-1865*, edited By W. C. Dodson, Historian (Hudgins Publishing Company, 1899)

William Joseph Hardee

Date	Events
October 12, 1815	Born in Camden County, Georgia
1838	Graduates from West Point (26th of 45); commissioned a second lieutenant in the 2nd U.S. Dragoons
1839	Promoted to first lieutenant
1840	Studies military tactics in France
1844	Promoted to captain
1846/48	Serves under both Zachary Taylor and Winfield Scott in the Mexican-American War
April 25, 1846	Captured at Carricitos Ranch, Texas (exchanged on May 11, 1846)
1847	Wounded at La Rosia, Mexico
1855	Authors *Rifle and Light Infantry Tactics for the Exercise and Manoeuvres of Troops When Acting as Light Infantry or Riflemen*
1856/60	Commandant of cadets, West Point
1860	Lieutenant colonel, 1st U.S. Cavalry
January 31, 1861	Resigns from the U.S. Army
March 7, 1861	Colonel, Confederate States Army; commander of Fort Morgan and Fort Gaines (Alabama)
June 17, 1861	Promoted to brigadier general
October 7, 1861	Promoted to major general
April 6, 1862	Corps commander at Shiloh, were he is wounded
October 8, 1862	Command of Left Wing of Braxton Bragg's army at the Battle of Perryville
October 10, 1862	Promoted to lieutenant general
December 31,	Corps commander at Stones River

Date	Events
1862 – January 2, 1863	
October 9, 1863	Jefferson Davis meets with Bragg and his Corps commanders (including Hardee), who give Bragg a vote of no confidence; Davis decides to leave Bragg in command.
November 25, 1863	Defeated at Missionary Ridge
January 1864	Marries Mary Foreman Lewis
May 1864 – September 1864	Sherman's Atlanta Campaign
August 31, 1864 – September 1, 1864	After fighting the Battle of Jonesboro under John Bell Hood, Hardee requests a transfer, and assumes command of the Department of South Carolina, Georgia, and Florida. After the War, Hood (unfairly) attributes the loss at Jonesboro to Hardee.
November – December 1864	One of the Confederate leaders who attempts to oppose Sherman during the March to the Sea, first from Macon, and then from Savannah
December 20, 1864	Evacuates Savannah, Georgia
March 19, 1865 – March 21, 1865	Defeated by Sherman at the Battle of Bentonville
April 26, 1865	Surrender to Sherman
1865	President, Selma and Meridian Railroad
1868	Authors *The Irish in America*
November 6, 1873	Dies in Wytheville, Virginia

William Hardee, a solid if not spectacular general, was born on October 12, 1815 in Camden County, Georgia. After graduating from West Point in 1838, two years later he would study military tactics in France.

In the Mexican-American War, he served under both Zachary Taylor and Winfield Scott. He was promoted twice, wounded once, and taken prisoner once.

In 1855, he put his French military knowledge to good use, writing *Rifle and Light Infantry Tactics for the Exercise and Manoeuvres of Troops When Acting as Light Infantry or Riflemen*, a book which was used on both sides during the Civil War.

William Joseph Hardee[10]

After joining the Confederate Army in March 1861, he quickly rose to the position of major general on October 7, 1861. A

---

[10] Library of Congress http://www.loc.gov/pictures/item/00652519/

year later, on October 10, 1862, he was promoted to lieutenant general.

He is most well known for serving as a corps commander under Braxton Bragg, a man that Hardee despised. On October 9, 1863, after Bragg had failed to pursue the Union army after driving them from the field at Chickamauga, Jefferson Davis met with Bragg and his Corps commanders (including Hardee), who give Bragg a vote of no confidence. Davis, however, decided to leave Bragg in command.

Hardee fought at Shiloh, Perryville, Stones River, Missionary Ridge, the Atlanta Campaign, and the Carolinas Campaign. He asked to be relieved of his command under John Bell Hood after the Battle of Jonesboro, a battle which Hood unfairly blamed Hardee for losing.

During the March to the Sea, Hardee bravely tried to defend the State of Georgia against Sherman's 62,000 troops, but Hardee never had more than 10,000 at one time. Hardee evacuated Savannah on December 20, 1864, allowing Sherman to occupy the city without a shot fired.

After the War, he served as president of the Selma and Meridian Railroad, and wrote a book entitled *The Irish in America* in 1868. He died on November 6, 1873 in Wytheville, Virginia.

Governor Joseph E. Brown

Date	Event
April 15, 1821	Born in Pickens, South Carolina. The family would later move to Union County, Georgia.
1844	Head-master of the academy at Canton, Georgia
1847	Opens law office in Canton, Georgia
1849	Elected to the Georgia state senate
1855	Elected state circuit court judge
November 6, 1857 – June 27, 1865	Governor of Georgia
1865/70	Chief justice of the Supreme Court of Georgia
December 27, 1870	Becomes president and part owner of the Western and Atlantic Railroad
1880s/1890s	Significant investor in the Dade Coal Company, which prospered through the use of convict labor
May 26, 1880 – March 4, 1891	United States Senator from Georgia
November 30, 1894	Dies in Atlanta, Georgia
1932	Joseph E. Brown Hall opens at the University of Georgia, Athens

Joseph E. Brown served as both senator and governor of Georgia, but is most famous for his time as the latter. He was a leading secessionist, and helped guide Georgia out of the Union on January 19, 1861. Brown served as governor of Georgia throughout the Civil War.

"Statute of Georgia Civil War Governor Joseph E. Brown and Wife, Georgia State Capitol, Atlanta, Georgia"[11]

Once Georgia had seceded, though, Brown would be a thorn in the side of Jefferson Davis throughout the whole War. As a strong believer in States' Rights, Brown generally refused to cooperate with the centralized Confederate government or even the Confederate Army. He opposed any attempt to draft Georgia soldiers into the Confederate Army, preferring them to be members of the Georgia State Militia. The Militia would see extensive action during Sherman's March to the Sea (most famously at Griswoldville).

---

[11] Creative Commons Attribution-Share Alike 2.0 Generic license. Photo by Ken Lund.

After the War, Brown would be involved in various business interests that might raise an eyebrow today from an ethics standpoint. A group led by Brown leased the state-owned Western and Atlantic Railroad in 1870, and Brown became president. Brown would become rich using convict labor to mine coal in Dade County.

Brown served as Chief justice of the Supreme Court of Georgia from 1865/70, and as U.S. Senator from Georgia from 1880/91.

Major General William Henry Talbot Walker

Date	Event
November 26, 1816	Born in Augusta, Georgia
1837	Graduates from West Point
July 1, 1837	Receives an appointment as brevet second lieutenant, 6th U.S. Infantry
July 31, 1837	Promoted to second lieutenant
December 25, 1837	Wounded in Lake Okeechobee, Florida during the Seminole War; appointed brevet first lieutenant
February 1, 1838	Promoted to first lieutenant
November 7, 1845	Promoted to captain
August 1847	Fights at the Battle of Contreras and the Battle of Churubusco (where he is wounded) in the Mexican War
August 20, 1847	Promoted to major
September 8, 1847	Wounded at the Battle of Molino del Rey (near Mexico City); becomes brevet lieutenant colonel
1854/56	Commandant of cadets at West Point
March 3, 1855	Promoted to major, 10th U.S. Infantry

Date	Event
December 20, 1860	Resigns commission in U.S. Army
February 1, 1861	Colonel, Georgia State Militia
March 13, 1861	Major general, 1st Division, Georgia Militia
April 25, 1861	Colonel, Confederate Army infantry
May 25, 1861	Promoted to brigadier general
October 22, 1861	Put in command of 1st brigade, 4th Division of the Potomac District of the Department of Northern Virginia, and resigns his commission soon after
November 1861/January 1863	Brigadier general, Georgia Militia
February 9, 1863	Brigadier general, Confederate Army
May 23, 1863	Promoted to major general
1863	Fights in the Vicksburg Campaign under Joe Johnston
September 19/20, 1863	Battle of Chickamauga (commands reserve corps)
July 22, 1864	Dies in Atlanta, Georgia, during the Battle of Atlanta
1916	Dedication of a bronze bust at Vicksburg National Military Park

Major General William Henry Talbot Walker served with distinction in the Seminole Wars, the Mexican War, and the Civil War. He was wounded multiple times while fighting in the Seminole Wars and the Mexican War, and earned the sobriquet *Shot Pouch*.

After resigning his commission in the United States Army on December 20, 1860, Walker would serve as a general in both the Georgia Militia, and the Confederate Army. He fought in the Vicksburg Campaign, commanded a reserve corps at Chickamauga, and served as a division commander under William Hardee during the Atlanta Campaign.

He was shot from his horse by Union pickets during the Battle of Atlanta on July 22, 1864, and died instantly. John Bell Hood later discussed the event in his *Memoirs*:

> I cannot refrain from mentioning the noble and gallant old hero, Major General W. H. S. Walker, who fell at the head of his division whilst bravely leading it into battle on the 22d of July. He was an officer of the old Army, had served with great distinction in the Mexican war, and was generally beloved by officers and men. On the night of the 21st, shortly before joining in Hardee's line of march with his troops, he rode by my headquarters, called me aside, and, with characteristic frankness, expressed his appreciation of the grave responsibilities attached to the position in which I had been placed; assured me that he full well understood the condition of the Army, after our protracted retreat from Dalton, and wished me to know, before he entered into battle, that he was with me in heart and purpose, and intended to abide by me through all emergencies. During the early afternoon of the ensuing day, I received the painful intelligence of his death; and I am certain that those officers and men who came within the sphere of his genial presence, will unite in the verdict that no truer or braver man ever fell upon the field of battle.[12] (John Bell Hood, *Advance and Retreat*)

---

[12] *Advance and Retreat*, by John Bell Hood (G. T. Beauregard, Hood Orphan Memorial Publication Fund, 1880)

Monument to Walker's death located near I-20/Glenwood, Atlanta, GA

Remains of Fort Walker in Grant Park, Atlanta, Georgia. This is the last remaining fort from the Battle of Atlanta. It was originally part of the 12 miles of fortifications that encircled Atlanta. It was designed by Col. Lemuel P. Grant (Grant Park).

Battles, Raids and Campaigns

Great Locomotive Chase

PULLING OUT OF BIG SHANTY.
"Pulling out of Big Shanty"[13]

The Andrews Raid was part of a bigger strategy on the part of Union Major General Ormsby Mitchel. Mitchel was in charge of defending Nashville, and he soon set he sights on Huntsville, Alabama and Chattanooga, Tennessee. Working with a civilian spy, James J. Andrews, a plan was formulated whereby Andrews would lead a group of raiders deep into the heart of the Confederacy in Georgia to steal a train north of Atlanta and steam north to Chattanooga. The goal – to destroy as much of the railroad and communications infrastructure between Atlanta and Chattanooga as possible, thus cutting Chattanooga off from assistance from Atlanta during the planned Union attach there.

---
[13] *Capturing a Locomotive* by William Pittenger (National Tribune, 1881)

"Portrait of Brig. Gen. Ormsby M. Mitchel, officer of the Federal Army"[14]

The plan was probably sound, however, the devil is in the execution. Most of the raiding party arrived a day late to the embarkation point for the raid, Marietta, GA. Thus, Andrews and his raiders were a day behind schedule. When the raid commenced on April 12, 1862, they were dogged by trains coming southbound from Chattanooga to Atlanta (as the Union offensive was already in full motion). Also, heavy rains made it impossible to burn the several wooden bridges along the W&A route between Atlanta and Chattanooga.

Andrews, a civilian, is a bit of a mystery. Andrews was a native of Hancock County, now West Virginia. He appears to have been a smuggler running contraband between the lines.

---
[14] Library of Congress http://www.loc.gov/pictures/item/cwp2003000359/PP

How he, as a civilian, ended up leading a military expedition behind enemy lines is not altogether clear.

William Pittenger, one of the Raiders, later described Andrews in this way:

> Mr. Andrews was nearly six feet in height, or powerful frame, black hair, and long, black, and silken beard, Roman features, a high and expansive forehead, and a voice fine and soft as a woman's. Of polished manners, stately presence, and more than ordinary personal beauty, wide information, great shrewdness and sagacity, he was admirably fitted to win favor in a community like that of the South, which has always placed a high value on personal qualities. He had also the clear forethought in devising complicated schemes, and the calmness in the hour of danger necessary for the perilous game he played.[15]

W&A script – dated April 1862

The *General* had arrived in Big Shanty at about 6:00 a.m. Most of the passengers (and all of the crew) left the train and headed to the Lacy Hotel for breakfast. It was at this moment that Andrews and his raiders struck. After uncoupling the passenger cars from the rest of the train, the three raider locomotive engineers and Andrews jumped in the cab, while the rest of the 16 raiders piled into the boxcars still coupled to the train. The *General* headed north, under the hand of

---

[15] *Capturing a Locomotive* by William Pittenger (National Tribune, 1881)

Engineer William J. Knight. Within seconds, the train crew began the chase on foot.

The raid entered into legend because the conductor of the train, William A. Fuller, and Western & Atlantic Railroad Superintendent of Motive Power Anthony Murphy pursued the stolen train for 87 miles, by foot, hand car, and three different locomotives, until the train was finally abandoned two miles north of Ringgold, Georgia.

Aftermath

All of the raiders were captured, with the following results:

- 8 were hung, including James J. Andrews
- 8 escaped, and made it back to Union lines
- 6 were involved in a prisoner exchange

Twenty of the 22 original military members of the raid received the Congressional Medal of Honor. As a civilian, Andrews did not receive the award.

The Great Locomotive Chase has been commemorated in numerous books, and at least two major Hollywood movies, including the 1926 *The General*, starring Buster Keaton, and the 1956 Walt Disney movie *The Great Locomotive Chase* starring Fess Parker. The first film on the raid was produced in 1911 by Kalem, a short silent movie named *Railroad Raiders of '62*.

In 1972, the *General* went on permanent display in the Kennesaw Civil War Museum (now the Southern Museum of Civil War and Locomotive History). The third of the pursuing locomotives, the *Texas*, is enshrined at the Atlanta Cyclorama.

After the raid, minor repairs were made on the *General* in Ringgold, GA. On May 2, 1862, the *General* was used to transport raiders from Swims Jail in Chattanooga to Atlanta.

"Buster Keaton in 'The General'"[16]

Sites associated with the Andrews Raid	Address or Location
Adairsville Museum	101 Public Square, Adairsville Georgia 30103
Allatoona Pass	Old Allatoona Road, Emerson, GA
Kingston Women's History Museums	13 E Main Street, Kingston, GA

[16] Library of Congress http://www.loc.gov/pictures/item/ggb2006005343

Sites associated with the Andrews Raid	Address or Location
Marietta Museum of History	1 Depot Street, Suite 200, Marietta, GA
Southern Museum	2628 Cherokee Street, Kennesaw, GA 30144
Tunnel Hill Visitor's Center	215 Clisby Austin Road, Tunnel Hill, GA

Chickamauga

"Battle of Chickamauga--Sept. 19 & 20, 1863--Federal ... (Gen. Rosecrans com.) Confederate ... (Gen. Bragg com.)"[17]

The State of Georgia had remained relatively unscathed by the Civil War until the Fall of 1863, when a great battle took place along an obscure creek in North Georgia called Chickamauga. From September 19-20, 1863, Confederates under General Braxton Bragg fought General William Rosecrans' Union army in one of the most brutal battles of the Civil War (Casualties: U.S. - 16,170; CS - 18,454).

In the weeks leading up to the Battle of Chickamauga, Bragg had been receiving reinforcements from Simon Bolivar Buckner, Joe Johnston, and James Longstreet. The largest amount of reinforcements were from Longstreet, Lee's highest ranking corps commander. Over a three week period, Longstreet shipped 15,000 of his men over 16 railroads from Orange Courthouse, Virginia to Ringgold, Georgia to reinforce

---
[17] Library of Congress http://www.loc.gov/pictures/item/91482113/

Bragg. The last two divisions of Longstreet's force arrived just as the battle of Chickamauga was beginning.

The shipment of the troops was slow and tedious because the South did not have standardized gauges for its railroads, forcing the troops to disembark as they moved from one railroad to another. Also, at the time of the shipment of troops, the Union held Chattanooga, so troops could not be routed to Chattanooga and then south on the Western and Atlantic.

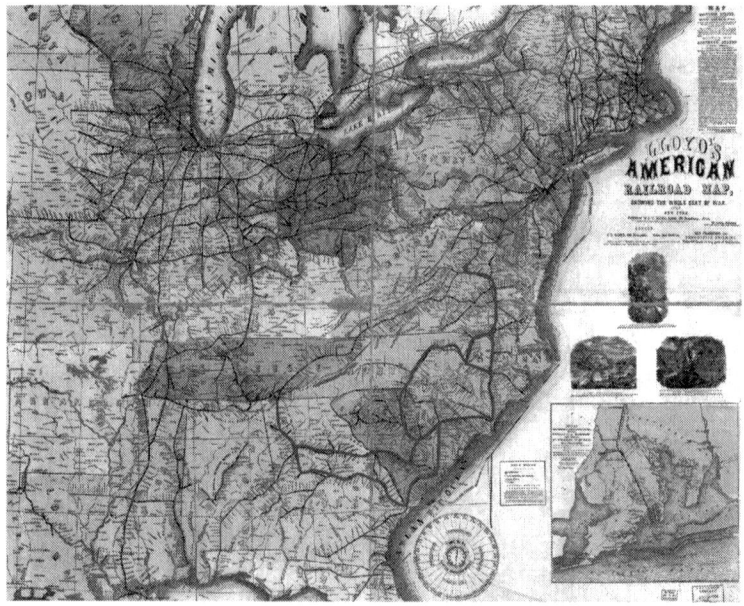

"Lloyd's American railroad map, showing the whole seat of the war", 1861[18] Superimposed on the map is the route of Longstreet's Corps.

---

[18] Library of Congress http://hdl.loc.gov/loc.gmd/g3701p.cw0014000

"Gen. James Longstreet CSA"[19]

Longstreet's shipment of so many men in such a short time via rail was a first in the history of the world.

Fighting at the Battle of Chickamauga after the first day was inconclusive, but on the second day, a poor command decision by Union commander Rosecrans led to a gap in the Union center. Confederate General James Longstreet, whose army had arrived on the battlefield by train from Virginia right before the battle, smashed through the gap in the Union center, and folded up the Union right. About a third of the Union forces (including Rosecrans) were driven from the field.

---

[19] Library of Congress http://www.loc.gov/pictures/item/cwp2003003004/PP/

Brotherton Cabin, site of Longstreet's famous frontal attack

Snodgrass Hill[20]

General George H. Thomas gathered Union forces on Snodgrass Hill, and through the afternoon and into the evening, successfully repelled 25 assaults from Longstreet. After darkness fell, Thomas ordered an orderly retreat from the field, heading back towards Chattanooga. Bragg's troops

---

[20] Library of Congress http://www.loc.gov/pictures/item/2004660063/

followed the next day, and occupied the heights south of Chattanooga.

Longstreet describes the moment when the Confederates took Snodgrass Hill, after Thomas had retreated:

> The contention by our left wing was maintained as a separate and independent battle. The last of my reserve, Trigg's brigade, gave us new strength, and Preston gained Snodgrass Hill. The trampled ground and bushy woods were left to those who were too much worn to escape the rapid strides of the heroic Confederates. The left wing swept forward, and the right sprang to the broad Chattanooga highway. Like magic the Union army had melted away in our presence. A few hundred prisoners were picked up by both wings as they met, to burst their throats in loud huzzas. The Army of Tennessee knew how to enjoy its first grand victory. The dews of twilight hung heavy about the trees as if to hold down the voice of victory; but the two lines nearing as they advanced joined their continuous shouts in increasing volume, not as the burstings from the cannon's mouth, but in a tremendous swell of heroic harmony that seemed almost to lift from their roots the great trees of the forest.
>
> Before greetings and congratulations upon the success had passed it was night, and the mild beams of the quartering moon were more suggestive of Venus than of Mars. The haversacks and ammunition supplies were ordered replenished, and the Confederate army made its bivouac on the ground it had gained in the first pronounced victory in the West, and one of the most stubbornly contested battles of the war.
>
> Our cavalry had failed to close McFarland Gap, and through that General Thomas made his march for the stand at Rossville Gap. The Union army and reserve had been fought, and by united efforts we held the position at Snodgrass Hill, which covered McFarland Gap and the retreat. There were yet five brigades of Confederates that had not been in active battle. The Confederate commander was not present, and his next in rank thought night pursuit without authority a heavy, unprofitable labor, while a flank move, after a night's rest, seemed promising of more important results. The Confederate chief did not even know of his victory until the morning of the 21st, when, upon riding to his

extreme right, he found his commander at that point seeking the enemy in his immediate front, and commended the officer upon his vigilance,—twelve hours after the retreat of the enemy's forces.[21]

Snodgrass Hill, where Thomas made his stand

Thomas was later referred to as the "Rock of Chickamauga" for his defensive stand at Snodgrass Hill. If not for the stand of Thomas, the Union army under Rosecrans might have been destroyed, delaying or making impossible Sherman's Atlanta Campaign in 1864.

The stand of Thomas, and the failure on the part of Bragg to pursue the retreating Union army took what might have been a great victory for the Confederacy, and turned it into a psychological victory for the Union.

---

[21] *From Manassas to Appomattox: Memoirs of the Civil War in America,* by James Longstreet (J. B. Lippincott Company, 1895)

The Rock of Chickamauga – George H. Thomas[22]

---

[22] Library of Congress http://www.loc.gov/pictures/item/cwp2003001167/PP/

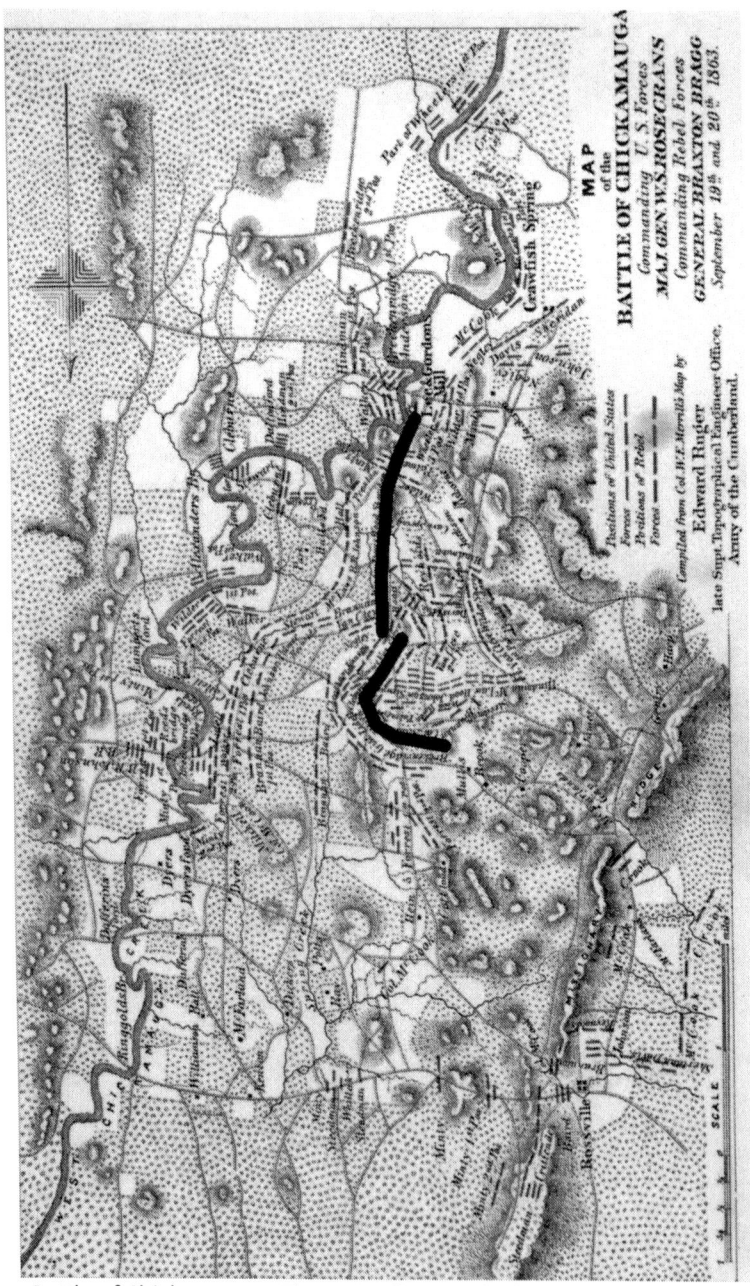

Battle of Chickamauga. The Union lines at the beginning of Day 2 are highlighted in black.[23]

---

[23] Library of Congress http://hdl.loc.gov/loc.gmd/g3866sm.gcw0102000

Battlefield	Address or Location
Chickamauga Visitor Center	3370 LaFayette Road, Fort Oglethorpe, GA 30742

Ringgold Gap

On November 27, 1863 at Ringgold Gap, Patrick Cleburne defended the Gap for five hours, allowing Bragg's Army of Tennessee to retreat successfully to Tunnel Hill. Cleburne and his troops were cited by a Joint Resolution of the Confederate Congress for their defense of Ringgold Gap.

The Battle of Ringgold Gap. Note the depot in the background. It was partially destroyed in the battle, and later repaired with a different color stone.[24]

---

[24] Library of Congress http://www.loc.gov/pictures/item/2004660818/

This modern photograph of the Ringgold depot shows the two shades of stones, with the lighter stones being used to repair the depot after damage incurred during the Battle of Ringgold Gap.

Sherman's Atlanta Campaign

> If the people raise a howl against my barbarity and cruelty, I will answer that war is war, and not popularity-seeking. If they want peace, they and their relatives most stop the war. (William Tecumseh Sherman)

The Atlanta Campaign of William Tecumseh Sherman has long fascinated historians and Civil War buffs alike. Many people consider that it was the first example of "modern" warfare. Sherman had some interesting and unorthodox (for the time) strategies and tactics:

- Sherman focused on winning his objective (Atlanta), rather than focusing on winning individual battles. Whether he won or lost an individual battle, he always continued on towards his objective (usually through a flanking movement).
- Sherman made every effort to keep his supply lines open, through the captured Western & Atlantic Railroad, but in

times when his troops needed to veer away from the railroad, they lived off the land.
- While the Atlanta Campaign was not as destructive as the ensuing March to the Sea, Sherman still wasn't shy about destroying as much of the Confederate infrastructure between Ringgold and Atlanta as he deemed necessary. When confronted by guerrilla activity at Cassville, Georgia, Sherman ordered the town burned to the ground in retaliation.
- One could also postulate that Sherman was an early advocate of using overwhelming force to accomplish a well-defined objective - no "contained warfare" for William Tecumseh Sherman!

Statistics		
	North	South
Strength	100000	74000
Artillery	254	124
Horses/mules	60900	
Wagons	5180	
Ambulances	860	
Casualties	31000	40000(?)

So why was Atlanta such an important objective for Sherman and the Union? Atlanta was both the supply and transportation hub of the whole deep South. In fact, Sherman based much of his strategy in the Atlanta campaign on the capture and/or destruction of four key Confederate Railroads, which spread at in spoke-like fashion from the Atlanta hub.

- Western & Atlantic (Chattanooga)
- Georgia Railroad (Augusta, Charleston, Richmond)

- Macon & Western (Macon, Savannah)
- Atlanta & West Point (Montgomery)

If Atlanta fell, it was only a matter of time before the rest of the Deep South fell with it.

The Atlanta Campaign started on May 6, 1864, when Sherman's vast army pulled out of its forward base in Ringgold, GA. The Campaign ended on September 2, 1864, when the heart of the deep South fell - Atlanta, GA. Sherman faced two Confederate commanders in the course of the campaign - Joseph E. Johnston, and John Bell Hood, who took command on July 18, 1864.

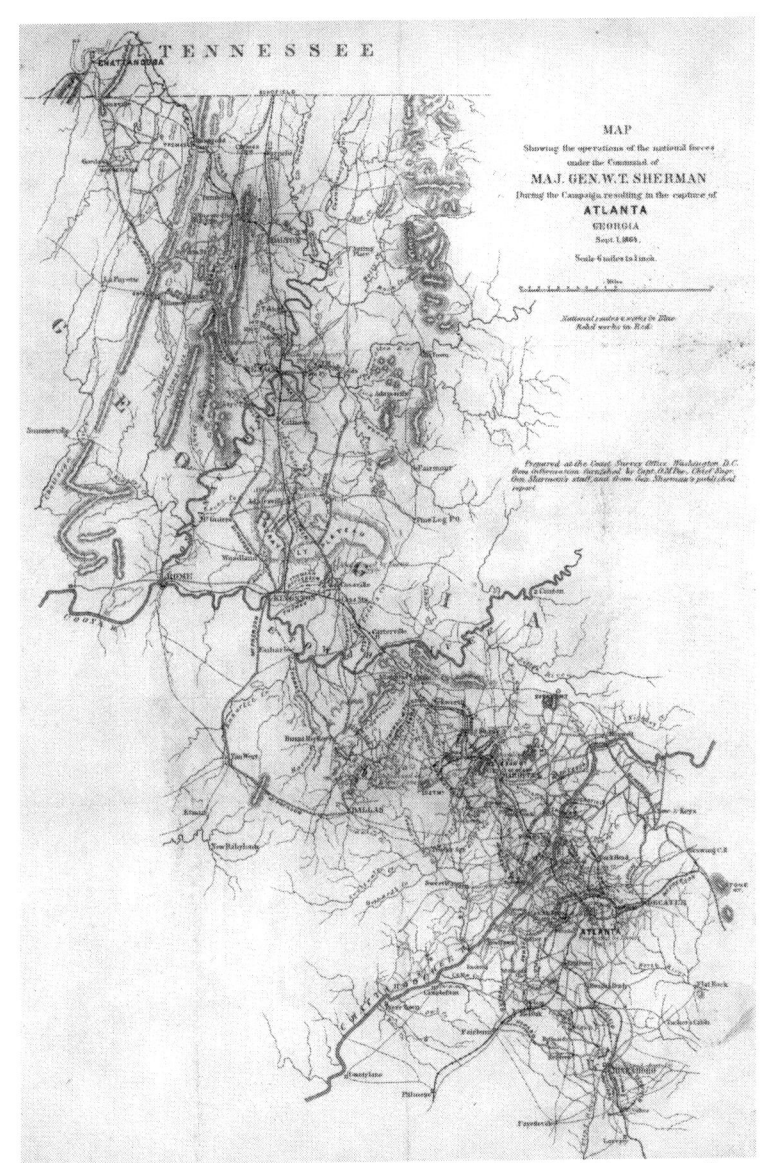

Orlando Poe map of the Atlanta Campaign, September 1, 1864[25]

The first two months of fighting occurred in North Georgia, north of the Chattahoochee River. Sherman actually lost most of the battles by traditional measures – in some cases, the

---

[25] Library of Congress http://hdl.loc.gov/loc.gmd/g3921s.cws00028

casualty numbers were more than 4-1 in favor of the Confederates. However, in each case, Sherman figured out how to flank Johnston, and continued towards Atlanta.

"Battle of Resaca--May 13 to 16, 1864"[26]

The greatest battle of the North Georgia phase of the campaign occurred in Resaca on May 14/15, 1864. While it was a Confederate victory, Sherman flanked Johnston, and continued towards Atlanta.

During most of the march towards Atlanta, Sherman kept close to his supply line, the Western and Atlantic Railroad. In late May, though, Sherman, wanting to avoid a head-on assault of Allatoona Pass, took his army to the west towards Dallas. It was during this detour that Sherman's forces suffered two of their worst defeats – at New Hope Church, and at Pickett's Mill. However, neither battle had any strategic importance, and Sherman eventually linked back up with his supply line in early June.

---

[26] Library of Congress http://www.loc.gov/pictures/item/91481351/

On June 27, 1864, Sherman attacked a strong Confederate defensive position at the Battle of Kennesaw Mountain, but was repulsed along a line of hills including Cheatham Hill, Pigeon Hill, and Little Kennesaw. The battle was a Confederate victory (US: 3,000; CS: 750/1,000), but by July 2, 1864, Sherman outflanked Johnston on the Confederate left, and resumed heading towards Atlanta.

Silent guns on Little Kennesaw Mountain

Battle	Date	Confed. General	Union Casualties	Confed. Casualties	Impact
Dug Gap	May 8, 1864	Johnston	350	150	Feint to allow McPherson's troops to infiltrate west of the mountains
Resaca	May 14-15, 1864	Johnston	6,800	5,200	Confederate victory, but Sherman flanked Johnston
New Hope Church	May 25,	Johnston	1,900	500	Some fighting occurred behind

Battle	Date	Confed. General	Union Casualties	Confed. Casualties	Impact
	1864				tombstones in the local Baptist cemetery
Pickett's Mill	May 27, 1864	Johnston	1,600	400	Sherman didn't mention this battle in his memoirs!
Kennesaw Mountain	June 27, 1864	Johnston	3000	750/1000	Confederate victory, but Sherman flanked Johnston

c. 1888 lithograph "Battle of Atlanta"[27]

As Sherman moved ever closer to Atlanta, Jefferson Davis made a fateful command decision on July 17, 1864, when he replaced Joe Johnston with John Bell Hood. This was probably a poor decision under any circumstances, but especially poor as Sherman was closing in on the defenses of Atlanta – Joe

---

[27] Library of Congress http://www.loc.gov/pictures/item/91482104

Johnston had a reputation for being a great defensive general, while Hood's reputation was on the offensive side.

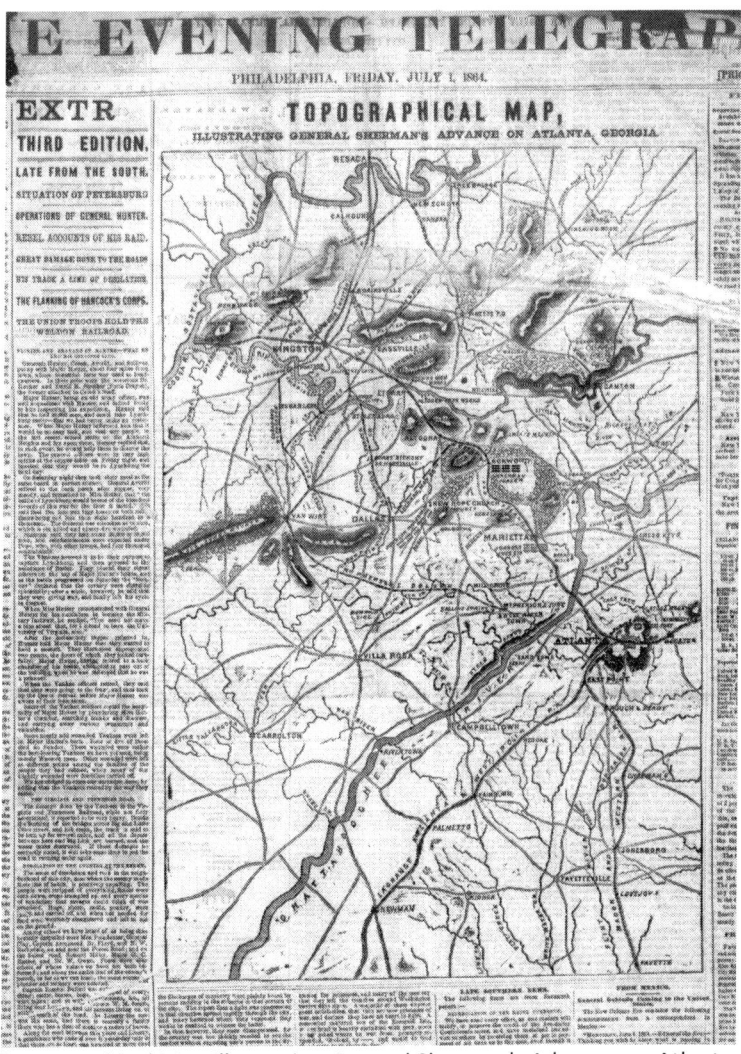

"Topographical Map Illustrating General Sherman's Advance on Atlanta, Georgia"[28]

---

[28] *The Evening Telegraph*, Philadelphia, Pennsylvania, July 1, 1864

The battles for Atlanta basically proceeded in a counterclockwise fashion as Sherman destroyed the railroads radiating from Atlanta like spokes on a bicycle. And while almost all of the battles against Johnston were Confederate victories in terms of the casualty numbers, this sharply changed almost immediately when Hood took over. The Battle of Peachtree Creek was a huge victory for "Rock of Chickamauga" General George Thomas, as was the battle immediately following it, the Battle of Atlanta, where the Union had a 2:1 advantage in terms of casualties.

Battle	Date	Confed. General	Union Casualties	Confed. Casualties	Impact
Peachtree Creek	July 20, 1864	Hood	1,800	2,500	Victory for "Rock of Chickamauga" George Thomas
Battle of Atlanta	July 21/22, 1864	Hood	3,700	7,000	The great battle between Hood and Sherman; McPherson is killed
Ezra Church	July 28, 1864	Hood	600	3,000	Fighting centered west of Atlanta, near the log Ezra Methodist Church
Jonesboro	Aug. 31 - Sept. 1, 1864	Hood	1,450	3,100	Sherman moved almost his whole Army SW to destroy the last remaining RR servicing Atlanta

By September 1, 1864, Sherman had cut off all of the supply lines into Atlanta, and prepared to take the city. Sherman describes the moment in his memoirs:

> Meantime General Slocum had reached his corps (the Twentieth), stationed at the Chattahoochee bridge, had relieved General A. S. Williams in command, and orders had been sent back to him to feel forward occasionally toward Atlanta, to observe the effect when we had reached the railroad. That night I was so restless and impatient that I could not sleep, and about midnight there arose toward Atlanta sounds of shells exploding, and other sound like that of musketry. I walked to the house of a farmer close by my bivouac, called him out to listen to the reverberations which came from the direction of Atlanta (twenty miles to the north of us), and inquired of him if he had resided there long. He said he had, and that these sounds were just like those of a battle. An interval of quiet then ensued, when again, about 4 a.m., arose other similar explosions, but I still remained in doubt whether the enemy was engaged in blowing up his own magazines, or whether General Slocum had not felt forward, and become engaged in a real battle.
>
> The next morning General Hardee was gone, and we all pushed forward along the railroad south, in close pursuit, till we ran up against his lines at a point just above Lovejoy's Station. While bringing forward troops and feeling the new position of our adversary, rumors came from the rear that the enemy had evacuated Atlanta, and that General Slocum was in the city. Later in the day I received a note in Slocum's own handwriting, stating that he had heard during the night the very sounds that I have referred to; that he had moved rapidly up from the bridge about daylight, and had entered Atlanta unopposed. His letter was dated inside the city, so there was no doubt of the fact. General Thomas's bivouac was but a short distance from mine, and, before giving notice to the army in general orders, I sent one of my staff-officers to show him the note. In a few minutes the officer returned, soon followed by Thomas himself, who again examined the note, so as to be perfectly certain that it was genuine. The news seemed to him too good to be true. He snapped his fingers, whistled, and almost danced, and, as the news spread to the army, the shouts that arose from our men, the wild hallooing and

glorious laughter, were to us a full recompense for the labor and toils and hardships through which we had passed in the previous three months.

A courier-line was at once organized, messages were sent back and forth from our camp at Lovejoy's to Atlanta, and to our telegraph-station at the Chattahoochee bridge. Of course, the glad tidings flew on the wings of electricity to all parts of the North, where the people had patiently awaited news of their husbands, sons, and brothers, away down in "Dixie Land;" and congratulations came pouring back full of good-will and patriotism. This victory was most opportune; Mr. Lincoln himself told me afterward that even he had previously felt in doubt, for the summer was fast passing away; that General Grant seemed to be checkmated about Richmond and Petersburg, and my army seemed to have run up against an impassable barrier, when, suddenly and unexpectedly, came the news that "Atlanta was ours, and fairly won." On this text many a fine speech was made, but none more eloquent than that by Edward Everett, in Boston. A presidential election then agitated the North. Mr. Lincoln represented the national cause, and General McClellan had accepted the nomination of the Democratic party, whose platform was that the war was a failure, and that it was better to allow the South to go free to establish a separate government, whose corner-stone should be slavery. Success to our arms at that instant was therefore a political necessity; and it was all-important that something startling in our interest should occur before the election in November. The brilliant success at Atlanta filled that requirement, and made the election of Mr. Lincoln certain.[29] (*Memoirs of General Sherman*)

Sherman's huge victory in Georgia in September 1864 paved the way for Lincoln's reelection as President in November 1864.

Sites Associated with the Atlanta Campaign	Address or Location
Dug Gap	2211 Dug Gap Battle Road, Dalton, GA 30720

---

[29] http://www.gutenberg.org/files/4361/4361-h/4361-h.htm#ch19

Sites Associated with the Atlanta Campaign	Address or Location
Allatoona Pass	Old Allatoona Road, Emerson, GA
Brown's Mill Battlefield	155 Millard Farmer Road, Newnan, GA 30263
Cyclorama	800 Cherokee Ave SE Atlanta, GA 30315
Gilgal Church	Near 667 Kennesaw Due West Rd NW, Kennesaw, GA
Griswoldville	"Griswoldville Battlefield is located east of Griswoldville in Twiggs County, Georgia, 10 miles east of Macon via U.S. 80 and Ga. Hwy. 57 towards Gordon on Baker Road."[30] From SR57, we turned north on Battlefield Drive, west (left) on Griswoldville Road, and right on Baker Road.
Kennesaw Mountain National Battlefield	900 Kennesaw Mountain Dr, Kennesaw, GA
Kingston Women's History Museums	13 E Main Street, Kingston, GA
Marietta Museum of History	1 Depot Street, Suite 200, Marietta, GA
Peachtree Creek	Collier Rd at Walthall Dr., Atlanta, GA
Pickett's Mill	4432 Mt Tabor Church Rd, Dallas, GA 30157
River Line Park (Shoupade remains)	6043 Oakdale Road, Mableton, GA 30126

---

[30] http://www.gastateparks.org/core/item/page.aspx?s=153653.0.1.5

Sites Associated with the Atlanta Campaign	Address or Location
Shoupade Park	4770 Oakdale Road, Smyrna, GA 30080
Southern Museum	2628 Cherokee Street, Kennesaw, GA 30144
Tunnel Hill Visitor's Center	215 Clisby Austin Road, Tunnel Hill, GA

1864 drawing of the battle at Dug Gap[31]

---

[31] Library of Congress http://www.loc.gov/pictures/item/2004660836

Rugged terrain at Dug Gap

Gilgal Church

c. 1891 lithograph - "Battle of Kennesaw Mountain"[32]

Illinois Monument at Kennesaw Mountain

---

[32] Library of Congress http://www.loc.gov/pictures/item/91482215

Portion of the Cyclorama, depicting the Battle of Atlanta[33]

---
[33] Library of Congress http://www.loc.gov/pictures/item/2011630674/

Wheeler Monument, Brown's Mill Battlefield, located on the corner of Old Corinth Road and Millard Farmer Road, south of Newnan.

Stoneman's Raid

> "It was a bold and rash adventure, but I sanctioned it, and hoped for its success from its very rashness..." (William Tecumseh Sherman, *Official Record*)[34]

On July 8, 1864, Sherman's forces under Brig. Gen. Jacob D. Cox's 3rd division crossed the Chattahoochee River, beginning a series of battles that would last until the fall of Atlanta on September 2, 1864.

Sherman knew that the way to take Atlanta wasn't to attack it head on (it was one of the most heavily fortified cities in the world at the time), but rather to cut off access to the four railroads which fed into Atlanta in a hub and spoke manner. The Western and Atlantic Railroad had been controlled by Sherman for weeks. The Georgia Railroad link had been severed because of Kenner Garrard's cavalry raid on the railroad bridges near Conyers and Covington on July 21/24, 1864. This left the Macon & Western (Macon, Savannah) and Atlantic & West Point (Montgomery) Railroads to destroy.

In late July 1864, Sherman ordered two of his cavalry commanders to launch a raid on the M&W Railroad south of Atlanta, concurrent with an infantry movement at East Point on the A&WP Railroad. Sherman describes the plan:

> I shifted General Stoneman to our left flank, and ordered all my cavalry to prepare for a blow at the Macon road simultaneous with the movement of the Army of the Tennessee toward East Point. To accomplish this I gave General Stoneman the command of his own and General Garrards cavalry, making an effective force of full 5,000 men, and to General McCook I gave his own and the new cavalry brought by General Rousseau, which was commanded by Colonel Harrison, of the Eighth Indiana Cavalry, in

---

[34] *War of the Rebellion: Official Records of the Union and Confederate Armies*, U.S. Government Printing Office, 1891

the aggregate about 4,000. These two well appointed bodies were to move in concert, the former by the left around Atlanta to McDonough, and the latter by the right on Fayetteville, and on a certain night, viz, July 28, they were to meet on the Macon road near Lovejoy's and destroy it in the most effectual manner. I estimated this joint cavalry could whip all of Wheelers cavalry, and could otherwise accomplish its task, and I think so still. I had the officers in command to meet me, and explained the movement perfectly, and they entertained not a doubt of perfect success.[35] (William Tecumseh Sherman, *Official Record*)

McCook's forces were to attack from the west, and Stoneman's from the east, meeting near Lovejoy's Station. A secondary, but perhaps no less important objective was to free Federal prisoners in Macon and at Andersonville, once the Macon & Western link to Atlanta had been severed.

At the very moment almost of starting General Stoneman addressed me a note asking permission, after fulfilling his orders and breaking the road, to be allowed with his command proper to proceed to Macon and Andersonville and release our prisoners of war confined at those points. There was something most captivating in the idea, and the execution was within the bounds of probability of success. I consented that after the defeat of Wheelers cavalry, which was embraced in his orders, and breaking the road he might attempt it with his cavalry proper, sending that of General Garrard back to its proper flank of the army.[36] (William Tecumseh Sherman, *Official Record*)

Stoneman's Raid was even less effective than McCook's, with Stoneman disobeying orders to meet McCook near Lovejoy's Station. Stoneman briefly attacked East Macon, and then retreated when he discovered that the Federal prisoners there had been transferred to Charleston. He returned via Sunshine Church (Round Oak), where he surrendered to a

---

[35] *War of the Rebellion: Official Records of the Union and Confederate Armies*, U.S. Government Printing Office, 1891
[36] *War of the Rebellion: Official Records of the Union and Confederate Armies*, U.S. Government Printing Office, 1891

much smaller Confederate cavalry force under General Alfred Iverson, Jr.

The following description is from *Appleton's Annual Cyclopedia for 1864*:

> On the 27th the two expeditions started forth, General Stoneman making for McDonough, a town about ten miles east of Lovejoys, and sending General Garrard to Flat Rock to cover his movement; and General McCook keeping down the right bank of the Chattahoochee. General Stoneman, however, almost immediately turned off toward the Georgia Railroad, which he followed as far as Covington, whence he struck due south and to the east of the Ocmulgee for Macon, distant sixty miles, in the neighborhood of which he arrived on the 30th.
>
> A detachment was sent east to Gordon, a station on the Georgia Central Railroad, where eleven locomotives and several trains loaded with quartermaster's stores were destroyed, together with several bridges between that place and Macon. But as he learned that the prisoners in Macon had on the previous day been sent to Charleston, General Stoneman decided to return at once by the way he had come, without attempting to reach Macon or Andersonville.
>
> On the evening of the 30th, he turned northward again, skirmishing on the way, and on the morning of the 31st, when about twenty miles from Macon, encountered a heavy force in his front. The country being unfavorable for cavalry operations, he dismounted a portion of his command and threw them forward as skirmishers, but soon found himself surrounded. After various fruitless attempts to make head against the enemy, he gave directions to the greater part of his force to break through the opposing lines, and escape in the readiest manner possible, while he, with several hundred men and a section of artillery, occupied the attention of the enemy. He was finally overpowered and compelled to surrender. Of his three brigades, one arrived safely within the Federal lines, one was attacked and somewhat scattered on the way back, and the third was captured with him. General Garrard, meanwhile, after waiting at Flat Rock for orders from Stoneman until the 29th, moved toward Covington, and

learning that he had gone south from that point, returned to his position on the left flank of the army.[37]

Sunshine Church II, built in 1880, replaced the church destroyed during Sherman's March to the Sea. General Stoneman was captured near here.

Sites Associated with Stoneman's Raid	Address or Location
The Cannonball House (struck with a cannonball during Stoneman's Raid)	856 Mulberry St, Macon GA 31201
Sunshine Church II	SR 11, Round Oak, GA

---

[37] *Appleton's Annual Cyclopedia* for 1864, vol. IV

Sherman's March to the Sea

After Ulysses Grant became head of the Union army in late 1863, one of his first acts was to put William Tecumseh Sherman in charge of attacking Georgia. Sherman felt that the civilian population of the Confederacy was as much responsible for the war as the Confederate Army. He pledged to make Georgia "howl".

Sherman had taken Atlanta, GA on September 2, 1864. In mid-November, he ordered the southern part of the Western Atlantic Railroad destroyed.

William Tecumseh Sherman[38]

---

[38] Library of Congress http://www.loc.gov/pictures/item/cwp2003003502/PP/

Sherman began his March to the Sea on November 12, 1864, when the destruction of Atlanta began. Sherman ordered everything destroyed except "houses and churches". Anything that could help the Southern war effort was destroyed – railroads, warehouses, manufacturing plants, public buildings, etc. Sherman's chief engineer Orlando Poe was in charge of the destruction, and used battering rams, fire, and explosives. Poe later estimated that 37% of Atlanta was destroyed; Southerners would later claim that the destruction was much more widespread, and included many private dwellings. Either way, it should be noted that few civilians were harmed – Sherman had evacuated civilians from Atlanta on September 7, 1864, weeks before he departed Atlanta for the March to the Sea. A Southern account of this evacuation follows:

> Add to all these horrors that most merciless and inhuman order of expatriation, by which the entire population of Atlanta, of all ages, sex and conditions, were driven forth to the fields of a desolated country, or shipped off to the rear like cattle; an order which was followed by the "deliberate burning of Atlanta" by Sherman's own account. But I have said enough about these horrors, for it is exceedingly unpleasant to speak of them. Yet they must be told, if for nothing else than to excite the execration of humane people, and they will be told more hereafter than ever before. It is not worth while to cry hush. The truth is entitled to be known.[39]

---

[39] *A Memoir of the Life and Public Service of Joseph E. Johnston*, edited by Bradley Tyler Johnson (R. H. Woodward & Company, 1891

Ruins of the W&A car shed in Atlanta[40]

On November 15, 1864, with his supply lines destroyed behind him, Sherman's forces began the fateful March to the Sea. Sherman had 62,000 troops split into two wings (the rest of his army was chasing John Bell Hood in Tennessee, under the command of George Thomas). The March, which took under a month, met little organized Confederate resistance. Much of the infrastructure of Central Georgia was destroyed along the way.

---

[40] Library of Congress http://www.loc.gov/pictures/item/2005681127/

c. 1868 engraving showing "Sherman's march to the sea"[41]

Sherman's goals during his March were to destroy the railroad and manufacturing infrastructure of central Georgia, as well as to take Savannah, and link up with Union supply ships in the Atlantic. To achieve this, Sherman, who had destroyed his supply line, the W&A, decided to have his troops "live off the land". It was through this decision that interactions between Union soldiers and Confederate civilians would take place.

Some excerpts from Sherman's Special Field Order 120 of November 9, 1864 show the rules for the Union forces.

> IV. **The army will forage liberally on the country during the march**. To this end, each brigade commander will organize a good and sufficient foraging party, under the command of one or more discreet officers, who will gather, near the route traveled, corn or forage of any kind, meat of any kind, vegetables, corn-meal, or whatever is needed by the command, aiming at all times to keep in the wagons at least ten day's provisions for the command and three days' forage. **Soldiers must not enter the dwellings of the inhabitants, or commit any trespass, but during a halt or a camp they may be permitted to gather turnips, potatoes, and other vegetables, and to drive in stock of their camp.** To regular

---

[41] Library of Congress http://www.loc.gov/pictures/item/2003679761

foraging parties must be instructed the gathering of provisions and forage at any distance from the road traveled.

V. **To army corps commanders alone is entrusted the power to destroy mills, houses, cotton-gins, &c.**, and for them this general principle is laid down: In districts and neighborhoods where the army is unmolested no destruction of such property should be permitted; but should guerrillas or bushwhackers molest our march, or should the inhabitants burn bridges, obstruct roads, or otherwise manifest local hostility, then army commanders should order and enforce a devastation more or less relentless according to the measure of such hostility. (emphasis added)
– William T. Sherman, Military Division of the Mississippi Special Field Order 120, November 9, 1864[42]

Sherman's foragers did not always follow the guidelines under section IV, especially the part about "Soldiers must not enter the dwellings of the inhabitants, or commit any trespass" – Sherman's troops often entered private houses, looking for items of value. Private houses were sometimes destroyed; rapes occasionally occurred (although these were probably mostly committed by "bummers" – disreputable men who followed along close to the army – rather than by Sherman's troops themselves.)

Sherman later commented:

A little loose in foraging, they "did some things they ought not to have done," yet, on the whole, they have supplied the wants of the army...

---

[42] *War of the Rebellion: Official Records of the Union and Confederate Armies*, U.S. Government Printing Office, 1891

"Sherman at Savannah"[43]

Again, a Southern view of the March is instructive:

> When Sherman cut loose from Atlanta, everybody had license to throw off restraint and make Georgia "drain the bitter cup." The Federal who wants to learn what it was to license an army to become vandals should mount a horse at Atlanta and follow Sherman's route for fifty miles. He can hear stories from the lips of women that would make him ashamed of the flag that waved over him as he went into battle. When the army had passed, nothing was left but a trail of desolation and despair. No house escaped robbery; no woman escaped insult; no building escaped the fire-brand, except by some strange interposition. War may license an army to subsist on the enemy, but civilized warfare stops at live-stock, forage and provisions. It does not enter the houses of the sick and helpless, and rob women of finger-rings and carry off their clothing.[44]

After taking Fort McAllister on December 13, 1864, Sherman's troops marched into Savannah unopposed on December 21,

---

[43] *The Sun*, New York City, December 16, 1864
[44] *A Memoir of the Life and Public Service of Joseph E. Johnston*, edited by Bradley Tyler Johnson (R. H. Woodward & Company, 1891

1864. He took Savannah a little over a month after leaving Atlanta. The Atlanta Campaign took four months to cover half the distance.

From a strategic standpoint the accomplishments of Sherman's March were prodigious:

- Sherman dealt a blow to the morale of the Confederacy from which it would never recover
- The March destroyed the railroads in central Georgia
- It split the Confederate forces still left in Georgia in half
- After taking Savannah, Sherman turned north for a march through the Carolinas in an attempt to crush the Confederates between his army and General Grant

Map of Sherman's March to the Sea[45]

Sherman discussed the impact of his March to the Sea on Georgia in the Official Report:

> I estimate the damage done to the State of Georgia and its military resources at $100,000,000 [multiple billions in today's money]; at least, $20,000,000 of which has inured to our advantage, and the remainder is simple waste and destruction. This may seem a hard species of warfare, but it brings the sad realities of war home to those who have been directly or indirectly instrumental in involving us in its attendant calamities. (emphasis added)[46]

---

[45] Public domain. Map by Hal Jespersen.
[46] *War of the Rebellion: Official Records of the Union and Confederate Armies*, U.S. Government Printing Office, 1891

After taking Savannah in mid-December, Sherman turned towards South Carolina and North Carolina. His tactics in those states were similar to his tactics in Georgia.

Leaving aside the moral argument, Sherman's actions in Georgia and the Carolinas were successful. He destroyed the infrastructure of central Georgia, and administered a crushing blow to Southern morale. After the fall of Savannah, and Grant's gains in Virginia, Southerners began to fear that the war was coming to a close against them.

1864 photo of "Interior view of Fort McAllister, 14 miles south of the city; the Ogeechee River beyond"[47]

---

[47] Library of Congress http://www.loc.gov/pictures/item/cwp2003000887/PP

Gun emplacement at Fort McAllister

Sites Associated with the March to the Sea	Address or Location
Fort McAllister	Near 3894 Fort McAllister Road, Richmond Hill, GA 31324
Fort Pulaski	US Highway 80 E, Savannah, GA 31410
Griswoldville	"Griswoldville Battlefield is located east of Griswoldville in Twiggs County, Georgia, 10 miles east of Macon via U.S. 80 and Ga. Hwy. 57 towards Gordon on Baker Road."[48] From SR57, we turned north on Battlefield Drive, west (left) on Griswoldville Road, and right on Baker Road.
Magnolia Springs State Park	1053 Magnolias Springs Rd, Millen, GA 30442

---

[48] http://www.gastateparks.org/core/item/page.aspx?s=153653.0.1.5

Sites Associated with the March to the Sea	Address or Location
Old Fort Jackson	1 Fort Jackson Rd, Savannah, GA 31404
Riverside Cemetery	1301 Riverside Dr, Macon, GA 31216
Rose Hill Cemetery	1071 Riverside Dr, Macon, GA 31201

Griswoldville Battlefield

Allatoona Pass

The Battle at Allatoona Pass happened after the fall of Atlanta, but before the March to the Sea, so it tends to get ignored in may histories of the Civil War. After Sherman took Atlanta on September 2, 1864, John Bell Hood took his troops north with the intention of disrupting Sherman's supply line, the Western and Atlantic Railroad. Between October 1-3, 1864, Hood's forces tore up fifteen miles of track near Acworth/Big Shanty, briefly retaking those cities, which had been captured by the Union during the Atlanta Campaign.

Hood then ordered Major General Samuel French with 3,276 troops to take Allatoona Pass, a heavily fortified railroad cut north of Acworth. The defending Union general, Brigadier General John Corse had slightly under 2,000 troops manning the two forts on opposite sides of the railroad cut.

The battle occurred on October 5, 1864. Some of the fiercest fighting of the whole War occurred there, with combined casualty figures over 30% (North: 706; South: 873). The fighting started early in the morning with a Confederate artillery barrage, and continued until mid-afternoon, when French's troops retreated.

The battle broke the back of John Bell Hood's plan to significantly disrupt Sherman's supply line from Atlanta to the north, and allowed Sherman to plan his march to Savannah with his Western & Atlantic supply line intact.

Both commanding generals referred to the battle in their memoirs:

> We crossed the Chattahoochee River during the 3d and 4th of October, rendezvoused at the old battle-field of Smyrna Camp, and the next day reached Marietta and Kenesaw. The telegraph-

wires had been cut above Marietta, and learning that heavy masses of infantry, artillery, and cavalry, had been seen from Kenesaw (marching north), I inferred that Allatoona was their objective point; and on the 4th of October I signaled from Mining's Station to Kenesaw, and from Kenesaw to Allatoona, over the heads of the enemy, a message for General Corse, at Rome, to hurry back to the assistance of the garrison at Allatoona. Allatoona was held by a small brigade, commanded by Lieutenant-Colonel Tourtellotte, my present aide-de-camp. He had two small redoubts on either side of the railroad, overlooking the village of Allatoona, and the warehouses, in which were stored over a million rations of bread.

Reaching Kenesaw Mountain about 8 a.m. of October 5th (a beautiful day), I had a superb view of the vast panorama to the north and west. To the southwest, about Dallas, could be seen the smoke of camp-fires, indicating the presence of a large force of the enemy, and the whole line of railroad from Big Shanty up to Allatoona (full fifteen miles) was marked by the fires of the burning railroad. We could plainly see the smoke of battle about, Allatoona, and hear the faint reverberation of the cannon.

From Kenesaw I ordered the Twenty-third Corps (General Cox) to march due west on the Burnt Hickory road, and to burn houses or piles of brush as it progressed, to indicate the head of column, hoping to interpose this corps between Hood's main army at Dallas and the detachment then assailing Allatoona. The rest of the army was directed straight for Allatoona, northwest, distant eighteen miles. The signal-officer on Kenesaw reported that since daylight he had failed to obtain any answer to his call for Allatoona; but, while I was with him, he caught a faint glimpse of the tell-tale flag through an embrasure, and after much time he made out these letters-" C.," "R.," "S.," "E.," "H.," "E.," "R.," and translated the message—"Corse is here." It was a source of great relief, for it gave me the first assurance that General Corse had received his orders, and that the place was adequately garrisoned. [49] (William Tecumseh Sherman, *Memoirs*)

I had received information—and General Shoupe [sic] records the same in his diary—that the enemy had in store, at Allatoona, large supplies which were guarded by two or three regiments. As one of

---

[49] *Memoirs of General William T. Sherman*, Volume 2 (Second Edition), by William Tecumseh Sherman (D. Appleton and Company, 1904)

the main objects of the campaign was to deprive the enemy of provisions, Major General French was ordered to move with his Division, capture the garrison, if practicable, and gain possession of the supplies. Accordingly, on the 5th, at 10 a. m., after a refusal to surrender, he attacked the Federal forces at Allatoona, and succeeded in capturing a portion of the works; at that juncture, he received intelligence that large reinforcements were advancing in support of the enemy, and, fearing he would be cut off from the main body of the Army, he retired and abandoned the attempt. Major L. Perot, adjutant of Ector's brigade, has informed me by letter that our troops were in possession of these stores during several hours, and could easily have destroyed them. If this assertion be correct, I presume Major General French forbade their destruction, in the conviction of his ability to successfully remove them for the use of the Confederate Army.

Our soldiers fought with great courage; during the engagement Brigadier General Young, a brave and efficient officer, was wounded, and captured by the enemy.

General Corse won my admiration by his gallant resistance, and not without reason the Federal commander complimented this officer, through a general order, for his handsome conduct in the defense of Allatoona.[50] (John Bell Hood, *Advance and Retreat*)

Both of the forts from the battle are still extant, one on top of each side of the Pass – the Star Fort, and the Eastern Redoubt.

The grave of the "unknown hero" can be found about 200 yards south of the entrance to the deep cut.

There is a small monument park to the right of the entrance into the deep cut.

---

[50] *Advance and Retreat*, by John Bell Hood (G. T. Beauregard, Hood Orphan Memorial Publication Fund, 1880)

Battle of Allatoona Pass[51]

Entrance to the battlefield

George N. Barnard photo of Allatoona Pass, 1864[52]

---
[51] Library of Congress http://www.loc.gov/pictures/item/2003663826
[52] National Archives and Records Administration, 533402. Public Domain.

About 200 yards south (just across the CSX railroad tracks) of the entrance to the railroad cut is the grave of a Confederate "Unknown Hero". The remains have long been assumed to be that of a soldier that fell at the Battle of Allatoona Pass, although that is only conjecture – the remains were shipped to Allatoona a few days after the battle in an unmarked wooden box. The original site of the grave was in the now abandoned railroad cut. The grave was moved to its present location in 1944, when the route of the railroad was changed.

Battlefield	Address or Location
Allatoona Pass	Old Allatoona Road, Emerson, GA

Training Camps

> I am requested to order the troops into camps of instruction, and am authorized by the Secretary of War to say that he will furnish them, at the expense of the Confederate States, with "clothing, equipments and arms," and that a bounty of fifty dollars will be paid to each volunteer private, so soon as his company is mustered into service, and that transportation will be furnished to each from his home to the place of rendezvous. The law also authorizes the volunteers to elect their own officers. In compliance with the request of the Secretary of War, I will establish three camps of instruction. One at Camp McDonald seven miles above Marietta, on the W. & A. Railroad; one at Camp Stephens, near Griffin; and one at Camp Davis, thirty miles from Savannah, on the Central Railroad.[53] (Joseph E. Brown, Executive Department, Milledgeville, Georgia, February 18th, 1862)

The first Georgia Militia training camps were established early in the War by Governor Joseph E. Brown, and included Camp McDonald at Big Shanty (Kennesaw), Camp Stephens and Camp Milner at Griffin, and Camp Davis near Savannah. Towards the end of 1864, with Sherman's forces sweeping across central Georgia, Governor Brown ordered the establishment of additional camps at Macon, Albany, Newnan and Athens.

> November 25th, 1864, Macon, GA
> It is hereby ordered, that a camp for organization of the militia of this State be established under my proclamation ordering a levy en masse at Macon, one at Albany, one at Newnan, and one at Athens, and that the militia report to the one or the other place as they may find it most convenient, with the least possible delay.[54] (Joseph E. Brown, Governor)

---

[53] *The Confederate Records of the State of Georgia, Volume 2* (Georgia Legislature, 1909)
[54] *The Confederate Records of the State of Georgia, Volume 2* (Georgia Legislature, 1909)

Camp McDonald/Phillips Legion

On June 11, 1861, Governor Joseph E. Brown established a training camp in Big Shanty (Kennesaw) for Georgian volunteers named Camp McDonald (after former Governor and Marietta resident Charles C. McDonald). The Camp included 60 acres of land west of the W&A railroad tracks. The Camp was commanded by Georgia Militia Brigadier General (and Confederate Army Colonel) William Phillips. Cadets from the Georgia Military Institute served as instructors.

The greatest moment in the history of the Camp occurred on July 31, 1861, when a Grand Review was held – some sources indicate that as many as 2500 men passed in review before Governor Brown. In the next several days, most of these troops marched off to Virginia.

Members of "Phillips Legion" fought in many battles, including Bull Run, Fredericksburg, Wilderness, Spotsylvania Court House, and Cold Harbor. After the war, several reunions were held by Camp McDonald alumni by the spring behind the modern day City Hall.

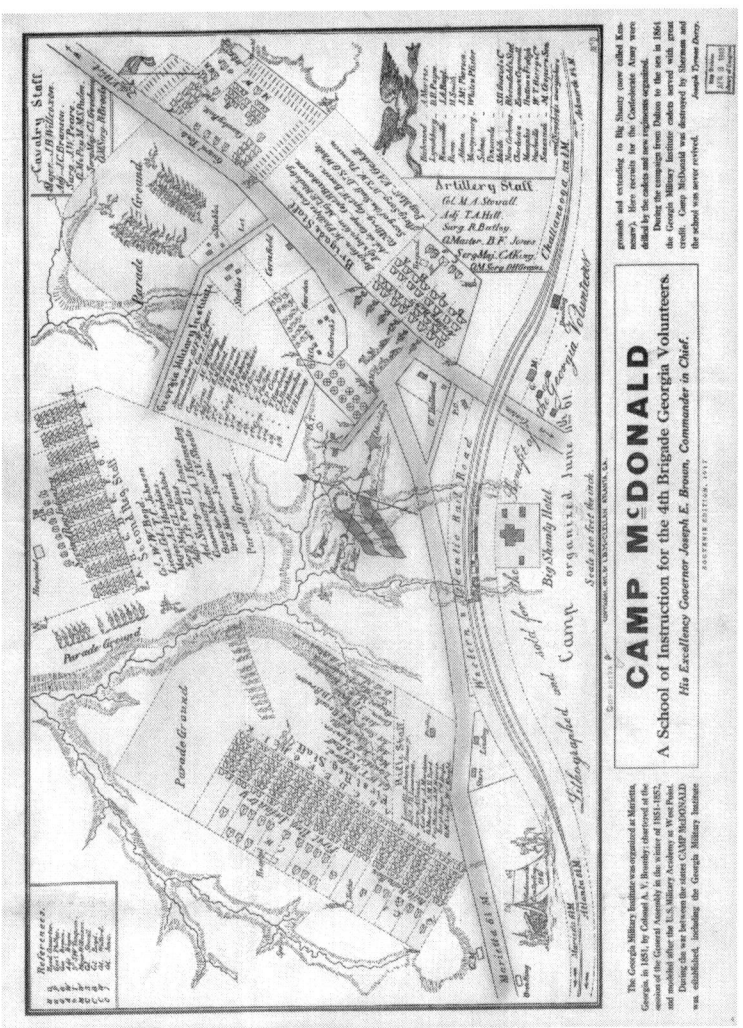

Map of Camp McDonald[55]

There are no remains of Camp McDonald today, as the camp was made up primarily of tents and parade grounds.

Camp Stephens

Camp Stephens, located in Griffin, Georgia, provided training to Georgia troops throughout the War. The camp was named

---

[55] Library of Congress http://hdl.loc.gov/loc.gmd/g3924k.cw0149000

after Alexander Stephens, Vice-President of the Confederacy. Nearby Camp Milner provided training for cavalry forces.

Joe Wheeler spent time at Camp Stephens during the retreat from Jonesboro and Lovejoy's Station, during Sherman's March to the Sea.

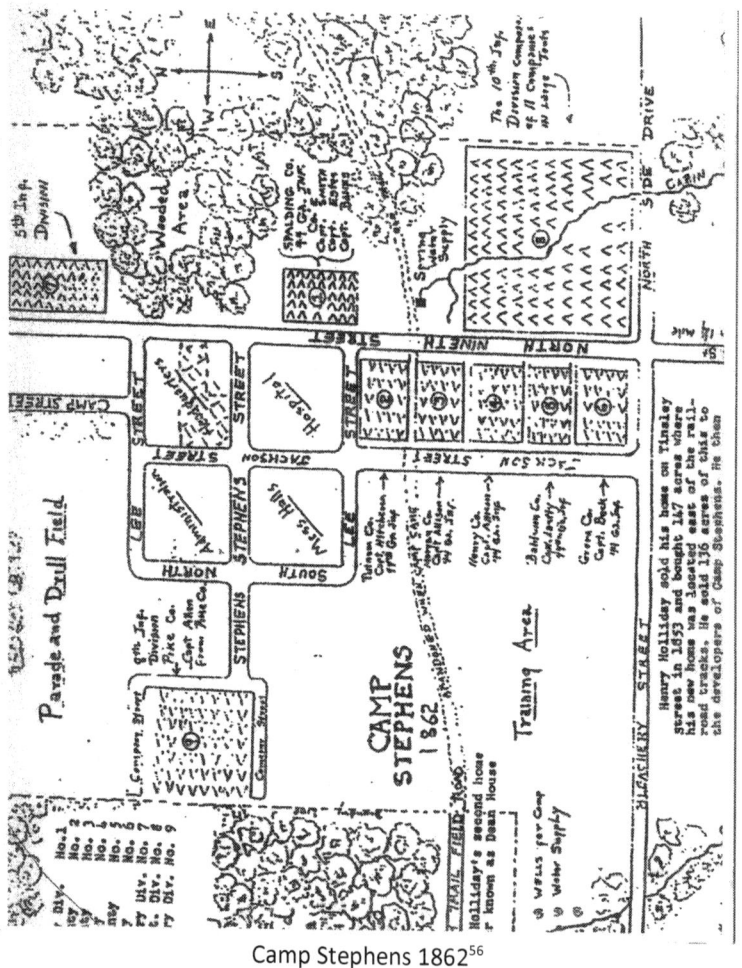

Camp Stephens 1862[56]

---

[56] Courtesy Holliday-Dorsey-Fife House in Fayetteville, GA

Camp Stephens today

Sites Associated with Civil War Training Camps	Address or Location
The future Camp McDonald Park is located behind Kennesaw City Hall	Near 2529 J O Stephenson Ave NW, Kennesaw, GA 30144
Camp Stephens	N. 9th and Stephens Sts., Griffin GA 30223

Forts

The most substantial forts in Georgia used during the Civil War are in the Savannah area. **Fort Jackson**, built between 1808 and 1812, was the anchor of the interior line defenses of Savannah. It was captured by William Tecumseh Sherman in December 1865.

Construction on **Fort Pulaski** began in 1829, and was at one time directed by Second Lieutenant Robert E. Lee. The massive brick fort in Savannah was seized by Georgia Governor Joseph E. Brown early in the Civil War. In April of 1862, a Union force with 36 guns, including the James Rifled Cannon, breached the walls of Fort Pulaski, and caused the surrender of the Confederate garrison there. The Union rifled cannon could shoot 4-5 miles, a huge advantage for an attacking force that didn't have to be in range of riflemen at the fort during an attack. The easy fall of Pulaski led to a radical change in fort construction throughout the rest of the War. New forts used earthen walls, which could easily absorb rifled cannon fire.

Fort McAllister south of Savannah is a good example of the aforementioned change in fort design. The complex fort has sloping earthen walls, which lessens the impact of cannon fire. As William Tecumseh Sherman closed in on Savannah during the March to the Sea, Fort McAllister became his prime strategic target. Fort McAllister was heavily fortified, but had only 200 troops manning it. On December 13, 1864, troops under General William Hazen stormed the fort, and took it in a battle lasting all of 15 minutes. Almost simultaneously, Sherman linked up for the first time with the Union navy. For all intents and purposes, Savannah was Sherman's for the taking.

There were other batteries and forts built in the Savannah area during the Civil War, including Thunderbolt, Rosedew and Tattnall.

"Thunderbolt Battery looking down the River"[57]

The remains of several small forts and batteries still exist at other locations in the state, including at Kennesaw Mountain, Allatoona Pass, Macon and Rome. One especially interesting set of fortifications existed on the Chattahoochee River north of Atlanta. They were known as Johnson's River Line, or the Chattahoochee River Line, and were the last major set of Confederate fortifications on the north and west side of the Chattahoochee River. The most prominent of those forts were 36 *shoupades*, arrow-shaped fortifications designed by Brigadier General Francis Asbury Shoup. Shoupades were linked by *redans*, upon which two cannon were mounted. The shoupades were 10-12 feet thick at the base, and 10-12 feet in height. They featured a walkway for infantry, and could accommodate up to 80 troops.

---

[57] Library of Congress http://www.loc.gov/pictures/item/2004661238/

The shoupades were intended to be a last-gasp defense against Sherman crossing the Chattahoochee. Like the Maginot Line in World War II, the invader simply chose to go around them. In Sherman's case, he crossed the Chattahoochee northeast of the Chattahoochee River Line, at the mouth of Sope Creek.

Georgia Civil War Forts	Address or Location
Allatoona Pass	Old Allatoona Road, Emerson, GA
Fort McAllister	Near 3894 Fort McAllister Road, Richmond Hill, GA 31324
Fort Pulaski	US Highway 80 E, Savannah, GA 31410
Fort Tyler	1111 W Sixth Ave, West Point GA 31833
Kennesaw Mountain National Battlefield	900 Kennesaw Mountain Dr, Kennesaw, GA
Old Fort Jackson	1 Fort Jackson Rd, Savannah, GA 31404
River Line Park (Shoupade remains)	6043 Oakdale Road, Mableton, GA 30126
Riverside Cemetery	1301 Riverside Dr, Macon, GA 31216
Shoupade Park	4770 Oakdale Road, Smyrna, GA 30080

Shoupade at Shoupade Park. The entrance to Shoupade Park is only five car-widths wide. It is nestled between two huge townhouse complexes.

Confederate artillery battery at Riverside Cemetery. The battery is (essentially) the "Pine Fort" section of the cemetery.

Fort Jackson, the anchor of the interior line defenses of Savannah

Interior of Fort Jackson

Sally Port of the Star Fort at Allatoona Pass

Damage to the walls of Fort Pulaski from Union rifled guns is still apparent after 150 years

Interior of Fort Pulaski today

Sleeping quarters at Fort McAllister

What rifled cannon can do to a brick fort[58]

---

[58] Library of Congress http://www.loc.gov/pictures/item/cwp2003000766/PP

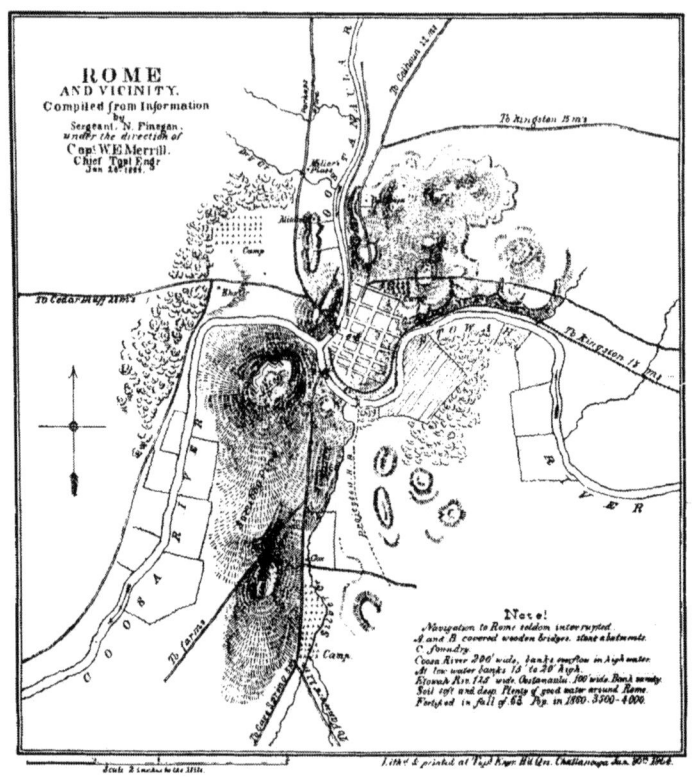

January 1864 map of Rome, GA. Rome boasted three forts during the Civil War.[59]

---

[59] Public Domain.

Manufacturing

> Georgia was no laggard in the march of progress, suddenly aroused from long slumber by the rude shock of arms, and taught in the school of adversity to turn her attention to other industries besides those of planting.[60]

This c. 1906 photo shows the the only remains of the Confederate Powder Works – the chimney from the Sibley Mill. The chimney still stands today, and has been recently restored.[61]

One of the areas in which the Confederacy was far behind the Union at the start of the Civil War was in manufacturing. While Georgia was welled served with 33 textile mills by 1861,

---
[60] *Georgia, Historical and Industrial*, by Obediah B. Stevens and Robert F. Wright (Georgia. Dept. of Agriculture, 1901)
[61] Library of Congress http://www.loc.gov/pictures/item/det1994013530/PP/

it was especially lacking in armaments and powder factories. The response, with the help of the Confederate Ordnance Bureau, was to establish a giant powder mill in Augusta, and establish a series of arsenals to produce bullets and the accompanying accoutrements. The arsenals existed in Columbus, Atlanta, Athens, Savannah, Macon and Augusta.

The **Confederate Powder Works** operated from 1862 to 1865, and produced 2,750,000 pounds of gunpowder for the Confederate war effort.[62]

During the Battle of Griswoldville on November 22, 1864, workers from the Confederate Powder Works and the Athens Arsenal served under Major F.W.C. Cook's Reserve battalions.

One of the reasons that Griswoldville was a target for Sherman's forces during the March to the Sea is because of the pistol factory located there during the Civil War. The factory was located in the old Griswold Cotton Gin Company plant. The first pistol was produced in July 1862. All told the plant produced 3,500 pistols for the Confederacy – a six-shot pistol, .36 caliber, with a 7.5 inch barrel. The factory was destroyed by Judson Kilpatrick on November 20, 1864.

Atlanta, with its plentiful water, trees and transportation options, was the key area in the State of Georgia in terms of various types of manufacturing. There are ruins of at least four manufacturing facilities in the Atlanta Metropolitan area, Including Sweetwater Creek (**New Manchester Mill**), Roswell (**Roswell Mills**), Sope (or Soap) Creek (**Marietta Paper Mill**) and the iron works at **Cooper's Furnace**.

New Manchester Mill, a textile mill, was established on the banks of Sweetwater Creek in 1849. The mill had five stories

---

[62] http://www.nps.gov/history/nr/travel/Augusta/sibleymill.html

and a 50,000-pound water wheel. The little town that once stood there had 500 inhabitants, but has since vanished.

Mill ruins in Sweetwater Creek State Park

There are significant mill ruins still extant, as well as the mill race.

Roswell Manufacturing Co. Mills (1839) manufactured textiles (cotton/woolen).

> The cotton and woolen mills at Roswell, on the Chattahoochee in Cobb county, were famous in the early fifties, their goods being held in high esteem and finding a ready sale in Tennessee, Alabama and Georgia. During the civil war the Roswell factory supplied good woolen cloth for suits for gentlemen and ladies.[63]

---

[63] *Georgia, Historical and Industrial*, by Obediah B. Stevens and Robert F. Wright (Georgia. Dept. of Agriculture, 1901)

Roswell Mills was burned to the ground by Kenner Garrard's cavalry on July 5, 1864. Five hundred women from Roswell & New Manchester Mills were resettled in Indiana by Sherman.

The Roswell Mill Machine Shop is still standing on the banks of Big Creek. Close by is the dam used to channel water power to Roswell Mills.

Marietta Paper Mills was established on the banks of Sope Creek in 1859, manufacturing various paper goods, including newsprint. On July 5, 1864, the mill was burned to the ground by Sherman's cavalry under Kenner Garrard. On July 8, 1864, the first Federal troops crossed the Chattahoochee at the mouth of Sope Creek

There are extensive mill ruins on both sides of the Creek. On the east side of Sope Creek, you'll need to hike about 200 yards to the ruins (easy path). On the western side, you can see the ruins from Paper Mill Road.

Mill ruins on the east side of Sope Creek

Cooper's Furnace iron works were established by Major Mark Anthony Cooper on the Etowah River in 1847[64], and manufactured pig iron. Cooper continued to run the facility until it was taken over by the Confederate government in 1862. It was destroyed by William Tecumseh Sherman on May 22, 1864. The old furnace still exists, but the supporting town of Etowah has vanished.

Cooper's Furnace is operated as a park by the Army Corps of Engineers.

Cooper Furnace

The **Atlanta Arsenal** operated from 1862 to 1864, and produced 46 million percussion caps and 9 million rounds of ammunition[65]. The **Atlanta Machine Works** produced parts for rifles.

---

[64] The Iron Works was initially developed by Moses Stroup
[65] http://www.georgiaencyclopedia.org/articles/history-archaeology/civil-war-industry-and-manufacturing

Macon contributed to the war effort with the **Schofield Iron Works** on fifth street, and the **Findlay Iron Works**, both which produced steam engines, among other items.

The **Columbus Arsenal** produced ammunition. **The Columbus Naval Iron Works** produced cannon for Confederate warships. Rome produced cannons for the Confederate Army, and Athens produced rifles.

This lathe is the only thing that survived the destruction of the Noble Foundry in Rome in November 1864 by Union troops. It is located at the Rome-Floyd Visitor's Center.

Double-barrel cannon on display at the Athens City Hall, produced at the Athens Foundry[66]

Sites Associated with Civil War Manufacturing	Address or Location
Athens City Hall (a double-barrel cannon produced at Athens Foundry can be found there)	301 College Ave, Athens, GA
Augusta Arsenal (now part of Augusta State University)	2500 Walton Way, Augusta GA 30904
Augusta Museum of History (contains a cannon produced at the Augusta Arsenal)	560 Reynolds St, Augusta GA 30901
Confederate Powder Works	1717 Goodrich St., Augusta, GA
Cooper's Furnace	River Rd., Cartersville, GA 30120 (on the Etowah River)
National Civil War Naval Museum at Port Columbus	1002 Victory Drive, Columbus GA 31901
New Manchester Mill (Sweetwater Creek State Park)	Near 1750 Mt. Vernon Road, Lithia Springs, GA 30122
Rome-Floyd County Visitor	402 Civic Center Drive, Rome,

---

[66] Public domain. Photo by Bloodofox.

Sites Associated with Civil War Manufacturing Center	Address or Location
	GA 30161
Roswell Mills machine shop	The machine shop and dam are in the Vickery Creek portion if the Chattahoochee River National Recreation Area, which is north of the Chattahoochee River in Roswell. A short hike is required from the parking area.
Sope Creek Parking Area	Near 3760 Paper Mill Road Southeast, Marietta, GA 30067

1864 engraving showing "Destruction of the depots, public buildings, and manufactories at Atlanta"[67]

---

[67] Library of Congress http://www.loc.gov/pictures/item/00652832

Hospitals

Hospitals existed in towns such as Ringgold, Dalton, Marietta, Forsyth, Newnan, Rome and Macon. As a matter of fact, almost every town of any size in northeast and central Georgia had at least one military hospital at one time or other during the Civil War. Sometimes more than one hospital would be located in a town (Newnan had four during Sherman's Atlanta Campaign).

Hospitals were located anywhere that could provide shelter, including courthouses, churches, private homes, tents, college dorms and classrooms, boarding houses and warehouses. In some cases, buildings were constructed for hospital use, such as the hospital complex under construction in Oxford (Covington), destroyed during Kenner Garrard's raid in July 1864.

> A large new hospital at Covington, for the accommodation of 10,000 patients from this army and the Army of Virginia, composed of over thirty buildings, beside the offices just finished, were burned, together with a very large lot of fine carpenters' tools used in their erection.[68] (Official Record – Kenner Garrard)

Most hospitals were mobile, and could be moved by rail or wagon on short notice, either to get closer or further away from the fighting. Individual hospitals (Newsome, Bragg, Gamble, Buckner, Quintard, Foard) would be moved as units, and set up in a new town or location. Thus, the "Bragg" or "Buckner" hospitals, for example, existed at multiple locations in Georgia during the War.

Hospitals in Georgia could have 1,000 patients or more. They were attended to by military doctors, and male and female

---

[68] *War of the Rebellion: A Compilation of the Official Records of the Union and Confederate Armies, The* (Government Printing Office, 1897)

nurses. At the beginning of the Civil War, many doctors resisted female nurses in the hospitals, but by 1863 to the end of the War, such female nurses were common.

Amputation was the common cure for sepsis, gangrene and other infections of extremities – there were no antibiotics in those days. Often all medical personnel could do was provide comfort until the inevitable death – not unlike hospice care today.

Field hospitals were usually in tents, and located very near battlefields. Bunks were "made of the branches of trees". Here, triage was done, and immediate care applied. Wounded soldiers would later be moved to more substantial hospitals, either by wagon or rail.

Soldiers who died in hospitals were typically buried in local cemeteries. This can be seen in many locations, such as Oxford (Covington), Forsyth, Newnan and Macon.

Local residents were not always happy to have a hospital established in their area, as such establishments often brought great disruption to the local community. Fannie Beers describes in her memoirs a foraging trip she went on into a remote area south of Atlanta, and how she faced suspicious residents who though she was going to steal her chickens.

Newnan Courthouse Square. The current courthouse was built in 1904. The whole courthouse square was used for hospitals during the Atlanta Campaign.

We get a real life look at what the Georgia hospitals were like from the memoirs of Confederate nurses Kate Cumming and the aforementioned Fannie Beers. Both described the hospitals in Georgia in some detail in their books, *A Journal of Hospital Life in the Confederate Army of Tennessee* (Cumming) and *Memories: A Record of Personal Experience and Adventure During Four Years of War* (Beers). Below are some excerpts from those two memoirs, listed by town.

Atlanta

We had concluded to return to Newnan, and as the cars did not start till 9 A. M., I visited one of the other hospitals, Dr. C. going with me; I think the name of it was the Medical College. The building is a very handsome one, and had just been fitted up. Every thing about it was in perfect order. It is one of the nicest hospitals in which I have ever been. It was filled with badly wounded men, as I am told is the case with every hospital in Atlanta. I found men there from every state in the Confederacy.[69] (Kate Cumming)

[May 1865] We saw many a field hospital. The bunks, made of the branches of trees, were left standing where the poor sufferers had lain, and where numbers of them had breathed their last. Near the hospital, the graveyards were to be seen, where, side by side, lay friend and foe. (Kate Cumming)

Rome

We took dinner, and were kindly entertained at the house of a very nice lady, a relative of Miss E. There we met an old lady who had been in the Quintard Hospital, in this place, and to judge from her conversation I should think that the ladies and surgeons did not get along very well together. From what I have experienced and seen, I expect there are faults on both sides.

---

[69] Text from *A Journal of Hospital Life in the Confederate Army of Tennessee*, by Kate Cumming (John P. Morton & Co., 1866); Photo from *Gleanings From Southland*, by Kate Cumming (Roberts & Son, 1895)

There are a number of hospitals in Rome, which are being broken up. As they seem to be very fine ones, and it is a healthy locality, I am always suspicious of some new movement taking place in the army when I hear of such things. (Kate Cumming)

Ringgold and Cherokee Springs[70]

Dr. Bemiss called early in the morning and took us through the hospital [at Cherokee Springs]. It is situated in a valley, and is one of the most lovely spots I ever beheld; I told Dr. B. it put me in mind of a picture I had seen of the "Dream of Arcadia." All around it had an air of perfect tranquility; it seems to me if the men get well any place they will here.

The hospital covers about thirty acres of ground, abounding in mineral springs, and in nice shady nooks.

We visited the wards; there are only three, although there are accommodations for five hundred patients; they are composed of tents, which are very tastefully arranged. Each ward is separate, having a wide street in the center, shaded by magnificent trees.

At present the hospital is filled with patients, a few of whom are sick enough to be confined to their beds; they are mostly chronic cases, sent here for the benefit of the water. (Kate Cumming)

The hospitals established at Ringgold, Georgia, early in the fall of 1862, received the wounded and the not less serious cases of typhoid fever, typhoid pneumonia, dysentery, and scurvy resulting from almost unparalleled fatigue, exposure, and every kind of hardship incident to Bragg's retreat from Kentucky. These sick men were no shirkers, but soldiers brave and true, who, knowing their duty, had performed it faithfully, until little remained to them but the patriot hearts beating almost too feebly to keep soul and body together. The court-house, one church, warehouses, stores, and hotels were converted into hospitals. Row after row of beds filled every ward. Upon them lay wrecks of humanity, pale as the dead, with sunken eyes, hollow cheeks and temples, long, claw-like hands...

Every train brought in squads of just such poor fellows as I have tried to describe. How well I remember them toiling painfully from

---

[70] Cherokee Springs was located about three miles from Ringgold

the depot to report at the surgeon's office, then, after being relieved of their accoutrements, tottering with trembling limbs to the beds from which, perhaps, they would never more arise. This hospital-post, as nearly as I remember, comprised only two hospitals, the Bragg and the Buckner. (Fannie Beers)

...The large brick courthouse in the centre of the town of Ringgold was especially devoted to my use. The court-room occupying the entire upper floor was fitted up for fifty patients. This was facetiously called "the nursery," and its occupants "Mrs. Beers's babies." (Fannie Beers)

In the midst of this terrible winter, on one of the most bitter days, there came about noon an order from "the front" to prepare for two hundred sick, who would be down late the same night. There was not a bed to spare in either of the hospitals. Negotiations were at once opened for the only church in Ringgold not already occupied by the sick. The people declined to give it up. But, "necessity knows no law;" it was seized by Dr. Thornton, the pews being taken out and piled up in the yard. Fires were then kindled in both stoves to thoroughly warm the church. There was, however, not a single bunk,—no time to make any; all the empty ticks when filled with straw and placed upon the floor fell far short of the number required. For the rest straw was littered down as if for horses, and when the pillows gave out, head-rests were made by tearing off the backs of the pews and nailing them slantwise from the baseboard to the floor, so that knapsacks, coats, etc., could be used for pillows.[71] (Fannie Beers)

---

[71] *Memories: A Record of Personal Experience and Adventure During Four Years of War*, by Fannie A. Beers (1888)

Tunnel Hill

At Tunnel Hill we saw a number of new hospital buildings; there were so many that they looked like a village. It does seem too bad that we are compelled to leave all of our hard work for the enemy to destroy.

The hospitals at the different stations which we passed were packing up to move. We think this bodes a very important move of General Bragg's. Some are hopeful and certain it will be a good one, while others are prophesying all kinds of evil. (Kate Cumming)

Newnan

The first thing we were told on our arrival was, that the citizens did not like the idea of the hospitals coming here. This seems strange; it can not be that these people have no relatives in the army, as we know how nobly Georgia has come forward at every call for troops; and have we not heard of their bravery on every battle-field in Virginia?

Well, if they have relatives in the army, do they not expect they stand a chance of being sick or wounded, and that, unless hospitals are provided for them, these same relatives would be in a terrible state, and denounce the government and everybody connected with it?

...Dr. Gamble and his surgeons have been out all day in search of hospital accommodations, and have succeeded in getting room for one thousand patients. They have taken nearly all the large buildings and stores. It astonishes me to see how cheerfully our men go to work again to fix up more hospitals.

...We have nothing arranged in the hospital, but it is filled with sick; many of them are on the floors. Mrs. W. and myself have two small rooms. One is used as a dining-room, sitting-room, and for making toddies, eggnogs, etc. A number of the officers we had at the Springs have followed us here, and they eat at our table for the present. They are to have a hospital set apart for them, as it is thought a better plan than having distinctions made where the privates are in the matter of rooms, and eating at separate tables. The doctors all seem to dislike having the care of them.

...The Coweta House is now a ward in the Bragg Hospital for the accommodation of Florida troops. Mrs. Harrison and a friend of hers, Mrs. Harris, from Florida, are its matrons.

...All the churches, with the exception of one, have again had to be taken for hospitals, and the young ladies' college besides. We have two very large sheds put up; one is on the court-house square. I like them very much for wounded, and the patients are all perfectly delighted with them. They have board roofs and tent-cloth sides, so as to be raised up or let down, as circumstances may require. They are twelve feet in width, and one hundred feet in length, with bunks arranged on each side, with an aisle in the center about five feet wide. I think this is the best arrangement that can be made for wounded in summer. They are well ventilated, and have none of the inconveniences of tents.

...A few days ago we received orders to pack up for a move. We were told to send the worst wounded to the Coweta House. As we have learned to do every thing with dispatch, all was ready for removal in a very short time. The cars were waiting for us, and the wounded who could be moved were put aboard. They disliked being left so much, that many pretended they were better than they really were. After every thing was in readiness, about dark, I went to the Coweta House to bid the patients good-by. The men had been sent from the Bragg, Gamble, and our hospitals. The galleries, halls, and rooms were full, and there were no nurses, no lights, and nothing to eat or drink, not even water. (Kate Cumming)

Meantime, the wounded of several battles had filled and crowded the wards. As before, every train came in freighted with human misery. In the Buckner Hospital alone there wore nearly a thousand beds, tenanted by every conceivable form of suffering. (Fannie Beers)

Besides the "Buckner," there were the "Bragg" and two more hospitals, the names of which I have forgotten, one presided over by two gentle ladies,—Mrs. Harrison and Mrs. ____, of Florida,—whose devotion and self sacrifice, as well as their lovely Christian character and perfect manners, made them well-beloved by everybody at the post. (Fannie Beers)

Macon

We reached Macon on the 6th, and I went to the Blind School Hospital, where my friend, Miss Rigby, is matron. It is a new hospital, and the building had been a school for the blind. It stands on a very elevated spot, and the view of the city from it is very fine. (Kate Cumming)

The Hooper-Turner house (1850s) near Mableton may have been used as a hospital

The 1828 Utoy Church was used as a hospital during the Battle of Utoy Creek

1860 Warren House, used as a headquarters and hospital by Union and Confederate forces. It has been refurbished since this picture was taken.

The Bailey-Tebault House, Griffin, Georgia, was used as a hospital

Entrance to Tift College, Forsyth, Georgia, used as a hospital in 1864

Some Sites Used as Hospitals	Address or Location
Bailey-Tebault House	633 Meriwether Street Griffin, GA 30224
Hooper-Turner house (owned by the City of Smyrna)	5811 Oakdale Road, Mableton, Georgia
Oxford College	100 Hamill St, Oxford, GA 30054
Tift College	315 Tift College Dr, Forsyth, GA 31029
Utoy Church	1465 Cahaba Drive SW, Atlanta, GA 30311
Warren house	102 W Mimosa Dr, Jonesboro, GA 30236

Headquarters

> ...my headquarters at Big Shanty, where I occupied an abandoned house. In a cotton-field back of that house was our signal-station, on the roof of an old gin-house.[72] (William Tecumseh Sherman, *Memoirs*)

"Exterior view of Meldrim house [Savannah] occupied by General Sherman as his headquarters" (1865)[73]

Like hospitals, almost every town in northeast Georgia had at least one structure that was used as a headquarters by Confederate or Union officers, sometimes just for a night, and sometimes for a number of months. Private houses and

---
[72] *Memoirs of General William T. Sherman*, Volume 2 (Second Edition), by William Tecumseh Sherman (D. Appleton and Company, 1904)
[73] Library of Congress http://www.loc.gov/pictures/item/2011648012/

boarding houses were the most popular, with senior officers getting the best accommodations.

"Atlanta, Georgia. Street in Atlanta (House next to church used as Sherman's headquarters" (George Barnard photo)[74]

---

[74] Library of Congress http://www.loc.gov/pictures/item/cwp2003005420/PP/

"Entrance Hall of Mr Chas. Green's house, Savannah Ga, now occupied as Head Quarters by Gen Sherman" (December 1864)[75]

"Headquarters of Gen. Geo. H. Thomas, Ringgold, Georgia"[76]

---

[75] Library of Congress http://www.loc.gov/pictures/item/2004661237/
[76] Library of Congress http://www.loc.gov/pictures/item/2012648417/

"Atlanta, Georgia. Federal officers standing in front of house. (Formerly headquarters of Gen. John Bell Hood.)"[77]

Clisby Austin House, Tunnel Hill (Photo by Lynda Bricker)

---

[77] Library of Congress http://www.loc.gov/pictures/item/cwp2003005431/PP/

This house may – or may not – have been Sherman's headquarters in Kingston. It can be found along the Rome RR wye in Kingston.

The 1840 Hamilton House was the headquarters of Brigadier General J. H. Lewis during the Confederate occupation of Dalton in 1863/64. The Huff House on Selvidge Street (location of an historical marker regarding Patrick Cleburne's call to arm the slaves) was the headquarters of Joseph Johnston. The Huff House is now the property of the Whitfield-Murray Historical Society.

The Acworth house of Confederate Captain James Lemon briefly served as Sherman's headquarters (or, perhaps, as headquarters of his staff), and was spared from destruction in November 1864 by a Union Major that had stayed there.

Buena Vista, the house the Wheeler used as a headquarters the night of July 30, 1864, after the Battle of Brown's Mill

Old Governor's mansion in Milledgeville, briefly used by Sherman as his headquarters

The Brown House in Sandersville, GA – Sherman slept here

Site of Rosecrans Headquarters, Chickamauga Battlefield

Some Headquarters Sites	Address or Location
Brown House	268 North Harris Street, Sandersville, GA
Buena Vista (private residence)	87 LaGrange Street, Newnan, GA
Clisby Austin House (used briefly by Sherman as a headquarters)	Near 215 Clisby Austin Road, Tunnel Hill, GA
Huff House	314 North Selvidge Street, Dalton, GA
Green-Meldrim House	14 W Macon St, Savannah, GA 13401
Hamilton House	701 Chattanooga Ave. Dalton, GA
Lemon House (privately owned)	Lemon Street and Willis Street, Acworth, GA
Old Governor's Mansion	120 S. Clark St., Milledgeville, GA
Warren house	102 W Mimosa Dr, Jonesboro, GA 30236

Prison Camps

There were several cities where prisoners were kept in Georgia during the Civil War, including Marietta, Macon (Camp Oglethorpe), Athens, Atlanta (Fulton County Jail), Savannah (Camp Davidson, plus a camp next to the city jail), Blackshear and Thomasville. However, the two most famous (or infamous) were the prisons at Andersonville and Millen.

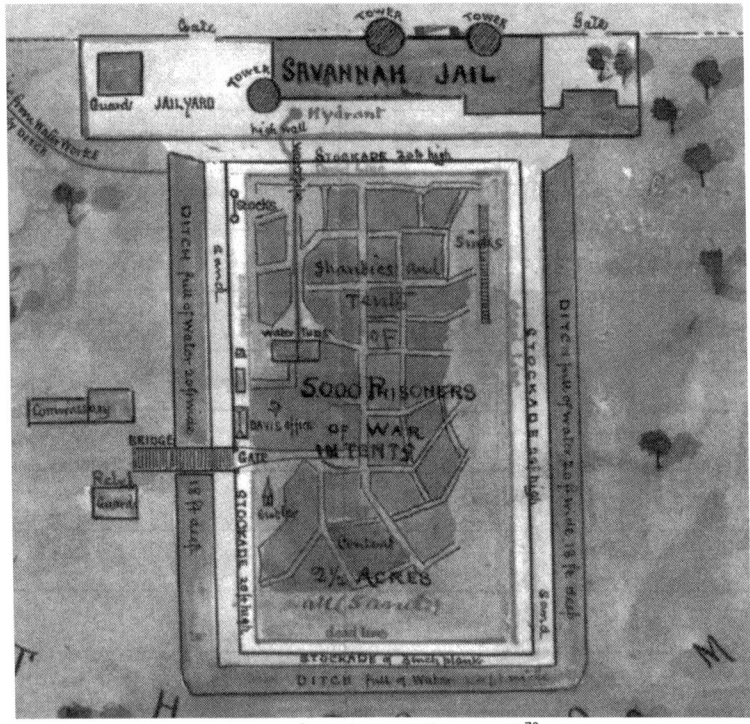

Map of a prison at Savannah[78]

Andersonville

Andersonville prison, located in southwest Georgia, was built by slave labor and opened in February 1864. It was built partially in response to the suspension of prisoner exchanges between the North and South in 1863, and also because the

---

[78] Library of Congress http://hdl.loc.gov/loc.ndlpcoop/gvhs01.vhs00304

South wanted to move prisoners out of Virginia from camps such as Belle Isle.

"Bird's-eye view of Andersonville Prison from the south-east"[79]

The camp included 27 acres, some of which was swamp. There were inner and outer stockades, and the beginnings of a third stockade, which was never completed. A (small) branch of Sweet Water Creek ran east/west through the prison, and served as the water source for the prisoners.

The original plan was to have barracks for 8-10,000 men. Most of those barracks were never built., and the few that were built were used as hospital space. Men not in the hospital lived outside, open to the elements, including the hot Georgia sun. Some built primitive dugouts, and covered them with tattered blankets or articles of clothing.

---

[79] Library of Congress http://www.loc.gov/pictures/item/2003662987/

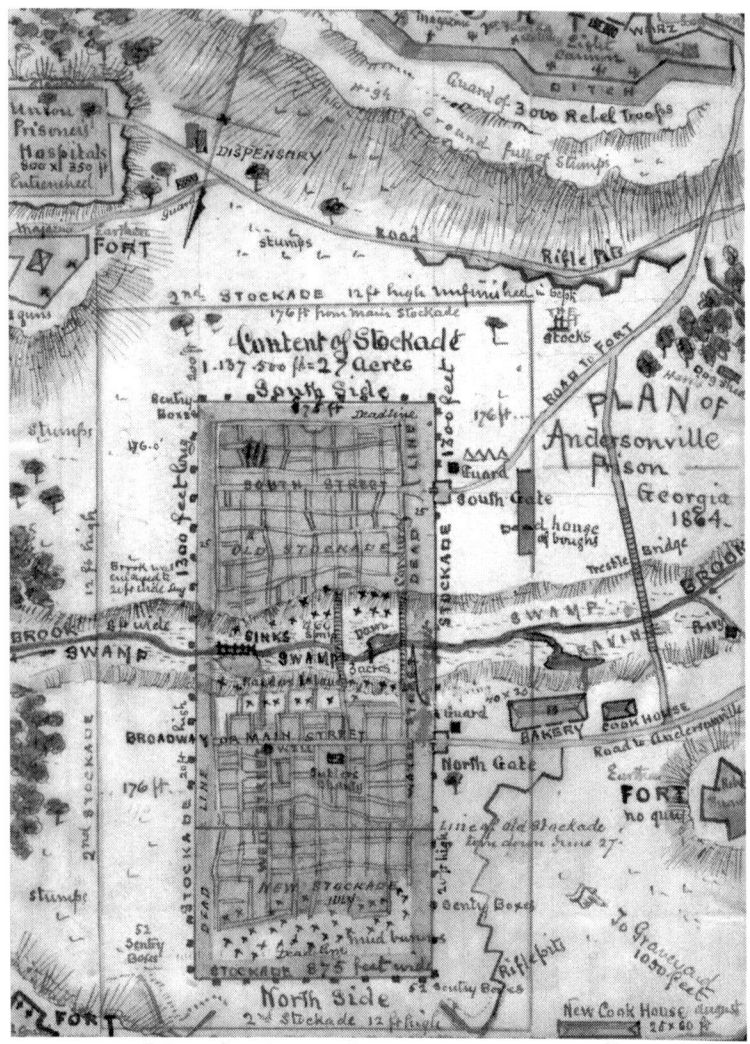

"Plan of Andersonville Prison, Georgia 1864"[80]

The number of prisoners soon sky-rocketed far above what the prison had originally been designed to hold:

March 1864 – 7,500 men
April 1864 – 10,000
May – 15,000

---

[80] Library of Congress http://hdl.loc.gov/loc.ndlpcoop/gvhs01.vhs00179

June – 22,000
July - 29,000
August – 32,899

By August 1864, Andersonville prison was the 5th largest city in the Confederacy.

Many of the 13,000+ men that died at Andersonville are buried in the cemetery next to the camp

Andersonville was also famous for its "dead line", an area where prisoners were told that if they walked into it, they would be shot. While many prisons had the equivalent of a dead zone, Andersonville is perhaps most famous for the concept, since (anecdotally at least) so many men were cut down in the forbidden area.

The Commandant of the prison was Captain Henry Wirz from Switzerland. At the beginning of the War, he was practicing medicine in Louisiana. He enlisted as a private, and eventually rose to the rank of Captain. He was humorless, had no empathy for the plight of the soldiers, and was probably completely overwhelmed with the job of running the largest prison camp on American soil in history. He was uniformly hated by the inmates.

Water source for 32,000 men

Conditions at Andersonville were appalling. Many hospital patients had to lie on bare floors. Along with malnutrition, common diseases and conditions included scurvy (or pellagra), diarrhea, dysentery and gangrene (there was no penicillin during the Civil War). Sewage often seeped into the water source. About a third of the prisoners died within 11 months. All told, about 13,100 prisoners died there.

As Sherman began plans for his March to the Sea in November 1864, most of the prisoners in Andersonville were transferred to Savannah or Charleston. About 5,000 sick prisoners remained. Conditions improved with a smaller number of prisoners.

Millen

Camp Lawton near Millen was planned by General John Winder in the summer of 1864 to relieve overcrowding at Andersonville. The site boasted plentiful water, had 42 acres, and was close to the Augusta and Savannah Railroad. Millen briefly had 10,000 prisoners in early November 1864, but it was evacuated on November 22, 1864 as Sherman's troops approached on the March to the Sea.

Brigadier General John Geary described the camp as it looked when Union troops captured it:

> About five miles north of Millen, and not far from the railroad, there is a prison-pen or stockade in which had until recently been confined some 3,000 of our soldiers. The stockade was about 800 feet square, and enclosed nearly fifteen acres. It was made of heavy pine logs, rising from twelve to fifteen feet above the ground; on the top of these logs, at intervals of some eighty yards were placed sentry boxes. Inside of the stockade, running parallel to it at a distance from it of thirty feet, was a fence of light scantling, supported on short, posts. This was the "dead line." About one-third of the area, on the western side, was occupied with a crowd of irregular earthen huts, evidently made by the prisoners. In these were lying unburied three of our dead soldiers, who were buried by us. Through the eastern part of the pen ran a ravine with a stream of good water. The atmosphere in the enclosure was foul and fetid. A short distance outside the stockade was a long trench, at the head of which was a board, bearing the inscription, "650 buried here."...This prison, if indeed it can be designated as such, afforded convincing proofs that the worst accounts of the sufferings of our prisoners at Andersonville, at Americus, and Millen were by no means exaggerated. (JNO [John] W. Geary, Brigadier-General, Commanding)[81]

---

[81] *War of the Rebellion: A Compilation of the Official Records of the Union and Confederate Armies, The* (Government Printing Office, 1897)

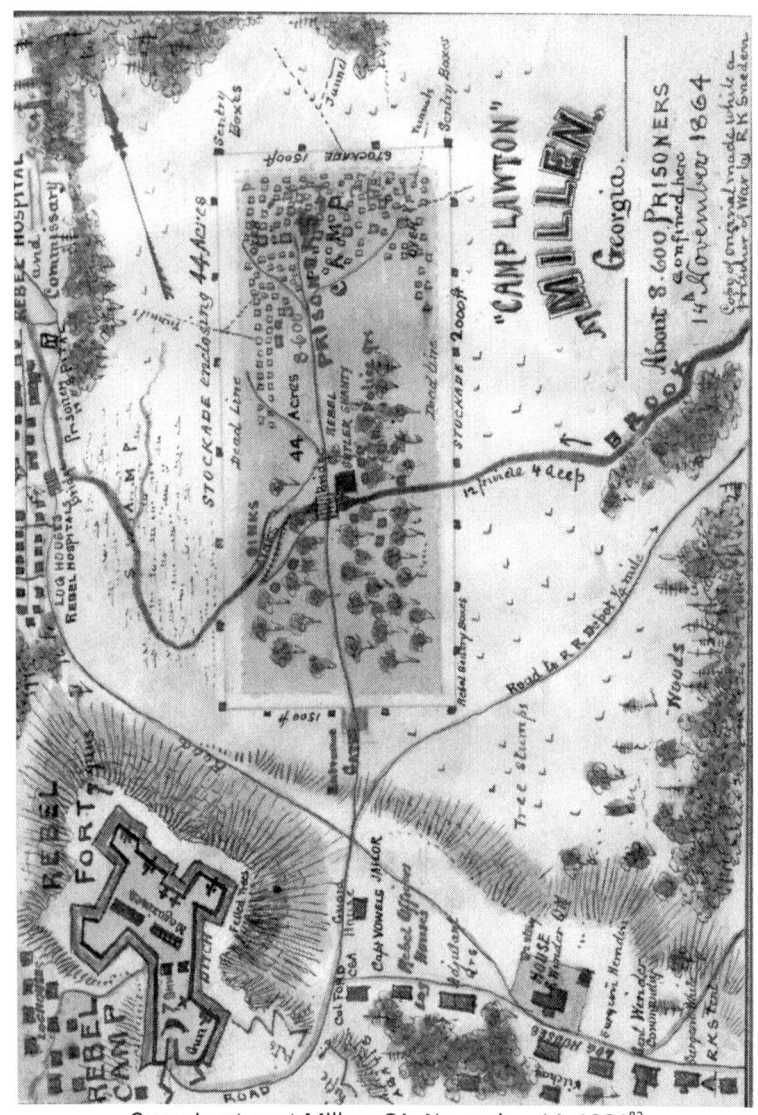

Camp Lawton at Millen, GA, November 14, 1864[82]

The remains of Fort Lawton, the Confederate Camp near the prison, are located within the Magnolia Springs State Park, about 5 miles north of Millen. The exact location of the prison camp has been lost for many years (the camp was

---
[82] Library of Congress http://hdl.loc.gov/loc.ndlpcoop/gvhs01.vhs00054

destroyed by Sherman's troops). In August 2010, students from Georgia Southern University announced that they had, indeed, found the site of the prison, located at the Bo Ginn National Fish Hatchery near the State Park.

Modern day remains of Fort Lawton

Prison Camps	Address or Location
Andersonville National Cemetery	760 POW Road, Andersonville, GA 31711
Magnolia Springs State Park	1053 Magnolias Springs Rd, Millen, GA 30442

Railroads

There were dozens of railroads in Georgia on the eve of the Civil War, but five would play an especially significant strategic role in the major battles and campaigns of the War in Georgia. They included:

- Western & Atlantic
- Georgia Railroad
- Macon & Western
- Atlanta & West Point
- Central Georgia Railroad

We'll take a brief look at all five, and their destruction by William Tecumseh Sherman in 1864.

Western & Atlantic (Chattanooga)

On December 21, 1836, the Western and Atlantic Railroad was born. The Georgia legislature authorized the building of a state-owned railroad from Chattanooga to Terminus, Georgia (now Atlanta). Companion legislation was passed by the Tennessee General Assembly on January 24, 1838, which allowed the railroad to be constructed into Tennessee.

By 1838, over 500 men (including some Cherokee Indians) were at work on grading, road bed, and trestles. In 1840, the original engineer on the project, S. H. Long, tendered his resignation after being criticized for slow progress. He would not be the last W&A engineer to resign for that reason.

In 1842, Charles Garnett was appointed the new chief engineer. More auspiciously, a wooden office was built in Terminus, cementing Atlanta as the future base of operations of the W&A railroad.

WESTERN & ATLANTIC RAILROAD.

W. L. Mitchell, Ch. Eng., Atlanta.   W. D. Fulton, Supt., Atlanta, Ga

Miles	Fares	ATLANTA to CHATTAN'GA. TRAINS LEAVE	1st Tr'n AM.		Miles	Fares	CHATTANGA To ATLANTA. TRAINS LEAVE	1st Tr'n AM.
		Atlanta*	8 30				Chattanooga	7 00
8	25	Bolton	9 00		11	30	Chickamauga	7 50
20	60	Marietta	9 50		20	60	Opelika	8 30
30	90	Moons	10 20		24	70	Ringold	8 45
35	1 05	Acworth	10 40		32	95	Tunnel Hill	9 20
40	1 20	Allatoona	11 00		40	1 20	Dalton‡	10 00
50	1 50	Etowah	11 25		48	1 45	Tilton	10 30
50	1 50	Cartersville	11 25		55	1 65	Resaca	11 00
55	1 65	Cass	11 40		66	1 80	Calhoun	11 20
60	1 80	Kingston†	12 20		70	2 10	Adairsville	12 00
70	2 10	Adairsville	1 00		80	2 40	Kingston†	12 40
80	2 40	Calhoun	1 40		85	2 55	Cass	1 20
85	2 55	Resaca	2 00		90	2 70	Cartersville	1 35
92	2 75	Tilton	2 30		90	2 70	Etowah	1 35
100	3 00	Dalton‡	3 00		100	3 00	Allatoona	2 00
108	3 25	Tunnel Hill	3 40		105	3 15	Acworth	2 20
116	3 50	Ringold	4 15		110	3 30	Moons	2 40
120	3 60	Opelika	4 30		120	3 60	Marietta	3 10
129	3 87	Chickamauga	5 10		132	3 95	Bolton	4 00
140	4 20	Ar Chattanooga.	6 00		140	4 20	Arr. at Atlanta*	4 30

* Connects at this point with Georgia R.R., see page 29. Macon & Western R.R., see page 31. Also, with Lagrange R.R., see page 32.
† The Rome R.R. diverges at this point, see below.
‡ Connects at this point with East Tennessee & Georgia R.R., page 53.
Stages leave Chattanooga, daily, for Nashville. Leave Cartersville for Rowland Springs. Tunnel Hill for Gordus Springs, during the summer months. Also, Two miles south of Ringold for Cotoosa Springs.
From Chattanooga, on Tennessee River, boats run tri-weekly, up to Knoxville, Tenn: and down to Decatur, Ala., daily, Sundays excepted.

April 1851 W&A schedule[83]

By 1845, the first 20 miles of track were in operation, allowing goods and passengers to travel from Terminus to the County Seat of Cobb County, Marietta.

On May 9, 1850, the first train traveled over the entire length of the W&A! The final cost of the railroad to the State of Georgia was $4,087,925.

The W&A RR is easily the most important of the five railroads in terms of strategic Civil War impact. For example, the last

---

[83] From *American Railways Guide for the United States* (Curran Dinsmore, April 1851)

leg of the transport of Longstreet's corps from Virginia to Chickamauga happened on the W&A.[84]

1849 W&A Tunnel Hill Depot

More importantly, the W&A served as Sherman's supply line for the Atlanta Campaign. Sherman would later make the following statement about the W&A:

> ...the Atlanta Campaign of 1864 would have been impossible without this road, that all our battles were fought for its possession, and that the Western and Atlantic Railroad of Georgia 'should be the pride of every true American' because, 'by reason of its existence the Union was saved'. (William Tecumseh Sherman, 1886, in a letter to Joseph M. Brown, son of the wartime governor)

On November 9, 1864, Sherman issued orders to destroy the W&A - from Big Shanty to the Chattahoochee, as he prepared for the March to the Sea.

> In accordance with instructions from Major-General Sherman, commanding Military DIVISION of the Mississippi, corps

---

[84] Many of Longstreet's Corps arrived at Catoosa Station on the first day of the Battle of Chickamauga, September 19, 2013.

commanders will have their commands in readiness to march at a moment's notice to commenced the complete destruction of the railroad...From Big Shanty to a point eleven miles south will be destroyed by the Seventeenth Army Corps, and thence to the Chattahoochee bridge by the Fifteenth Corps. The destruction will be most complete, the ties burned, rails twisted, &c., as [has] been done heretofore.[85]

During the destruction of Atlanta, W&A infrastructure was especially hit, with the destruction of track, rolling stock, the W&A train shed, and the W&A roundhouse.

After the War in 1870, the State of Georgia decided that it no longer wanted to be in the railroad business, passing legislation that required the leasing of the W&A (the State of Georgia would continue to own the right of way, as it does today). On December 27, 1870, a group led by former governor Joseph E. Brown won the first lease of the W&A. The lease was for 20 years, for $25,000/month.

On December 27, 1890, the W&A was leased by the Nashville, Chattanooga & St. Louis Railway (NC&StL), although it continued to operate under the Western & Atlantic name until 1919, when it became the "Atlanta Division of the NC&STL RY". The NC&StL lease was for 29 years at $35,001/month. Essentially, the W&A as an independent entity had ceased to exist in 1890.

---

[85] *War of the Rebellion: Official Records of the Union and Confederate Armies*, U.S. Government Printing Office, 1891

Georgia Railroad (Augusta, Charleston, Richmond)

The Georgia Railroad came into being in 1834, to provide a linkage with the South Carolina Canal and RR Co., which had run its tracks into Hamburg, South Carolina, just across the river from Augusta, Georgia. One of the smart decisions made early in the game was to name 26-year old John Edgar Thomson as Chief Engineer. Thomson would later go on to fame and glory as Chief Engineer and President of the Pennsylvania Railroad.

Thomson began surveying in late 1834, and had started grading by 1835. Concurrently, on the business side, the directors of the Georgia Railroad received permission from the Georgia Legislature to go into the banking business. The Georgia Railroad Bank was charted on December 18, 1835.

By the summer of 1837, the Georgia Railroad had proceeded 38 miles west of Augusta, to a town which quickly changed its name to Thomson, in honor of the Chief Engineer of the line.

By late 1841, the line was finished westward to Madison. Some time around that point, the decision was made to continue the line all the way to Terminus, the southern end of the W&A RR. The line from Augusta to Terminus (now named Marthasville) was completed on September 14, 1845 (five years before the first train would run from Atlanta to Chattanooga). Legend says that it was John Edgar Thomson who decided to rename Marthasville to Atlanta, perhaps because Marthasville was too long for railroad paperwork purposes.

GEORGIA RAILROAD.

J. P. King, Pres., Augusta.   F. C. Arms, Supt., Augusta, Ga.

Miles	Fares	F'm AUGUSTA To ATLANTA. TRAINS LEAVE	1st Tr'n P.M.		Miles	Fares	F'm ATLANTA To AUGUSTA. TRAINS LEAVE	1st Tr'n P.M.
		Augusta*.......	8 30				Atlanta†.......	5 00
11	30	Bel Air.........	9 10		6	20	Decatur........	5 20
21	60	Berzelia........	9 50		15	50	Stone Mountain	5 55
29	90	Dearing........	10 25		24	70	Lithonia.......	6 25
38	1 20	Thomson.......	11 05		30	90	Conyers........	6 50
47	1 40	Camak.........	11 45		41	1 20	Covington......	7 25
		Leave Camak.	1 00		51	1 50	Social Circle	8 25
4	10	Ar Warrenton	1 30		67	2 00	Madison........	9 25
57	1 70	Cumming......	12 15		87	2 60	Greensboro.....	10 35
65	2 00	Crawfordville..	12 50		95	2 80	Union Point...	11 05
76	2 30	Union Point....	1 40				Leave Athens	2 00
		L've U. Point	2 00		17	50	Lexington...	
5	10	Woodville...			27	80	Maxey's.....	
13	40	Maxey's.....			35	1 10	Woodville...	
23	70	Lexington...			40	1 20	Ar U. Point..	5 45
40	1 20	Arr at Athens	6 00		106	3 20	Crawfordville..	11 50
84	2 50	Greensboro.....	2 10		114	3 40	Cumming.......	12 15
104	3 10	Madison........	3 25		124	3 70	Camak..........	1 00
120	3 60	Social Circle	4 25				L've Warrent'n	11 00
130	3 90	Covington......	5 10		4	10	Ar at Camak.	11 30
141	4 20	Conyers........	5 55		133	4 00	Thomson.......	1 40
147	4 40	Lithonia.......	6 20		142	4 30	Dearing........	2 20
156	4 70	Stone Mountain.	6 55		150	4 50	Berzelia.......	2 45
165	5 00	Decatur........	7 25		160	4 80	Bel Air........	3 25
171	5 00	Arr at Atlanta†..	7 50		171	5 00	Arr at Augusta*.	4 00

* Connects at this point with the South Carolina Railroad, see page 28
† Connects with the Macon & Western R.R. at this point, see page 31.
Western & Atlantic R.R., see page 32. Also, Lagrange R.R., see page 61.
Stages leave Augusta for Clarksville, Gillisonville, Greensville, etc.
Stages connect with this road between Warrenton and Milledgeville, daily; and leave Athens every Tuesday, Thursday and Saturday for Gainesville, Clarksville, and Dahlonega.

1851 Georgia RR Schedule[86]

John Edgar Thomson left the GA RR in April 1847 to become Chief Engineer of the Pennsylvania Railroad. He became president of the PRR in 1852, and stayed in that position until 1874.

The Georgia Railroad, of course, was one of the transportation spokes on the wheel with Atlanta at the center, which Sherman wanted to sever during the Atlanta Campaign. This was accomplished somewhat spectacularly by

---

[86] From *American Railways Guide for the United States* (Curran Dinsmore, April 1851)

Union cavalry general Kenner Garrard, when he destroyed two key bridges over the Yellow and Alcovy Rivers on the Georgia Railroad in a series of raids from July 21/24, 1864. From the *Official Record*:

> Results: Three road bridges and one railroad bridge (555 feet in length) over the Yellow River, and one road and one railroad bridge (250 feet in length) over the Ulafauhachee, were burned; six miles of railroad track between the rivers were well destroyed.
>
> The depot and considerable quantity of Quartermasters' and commissary stores at Covington were burned. One train and locomotive captured at Conyers and burned; one train (platform) was burned at Covington, and a small train (baggage) at station near the Ulafauhachee, captured and burned...Citizens report a passenger train and a construction train, both with engines, cut off between Stone Mountain and Yellow River. Over 2,000 bales of cotton were burned.
>
> A large new hospital at Covington, for the accommodation of 10,000 patients from this army and the Army of Virginia, composed of over thirty buildings, beside the offices just finished, were burned, together with a very large lot of fine carpenters' tools used in their erection.[87] (Kenner Garrard, *Official Record*)

Damage was also done to the Georgia RR during the March to the Sea:

> The Twentieth Corps destroyed the Augusta railroad from Social Circle to a point near Greensborough, the Fourteenth Corps destroying from Lithonia to Social Circle. (O. M. Poe, Captain of Engineers, Chief Engineer Mil. Div. of the Mississippi.)[88]
>
> At Rutledge, Madison, Eatonton, Milledgeville, Davisborough, machine-shops, turn-tables, depots, water-tanks, and much other valuable property were destroyed. The quantity of cotton destroyed is estimated by my subordinate commanders at 17,000

---

[87] *War of the Rebellion: Official Records of the Union and Confederate Armies*, U.S. Government Printing Office, 1891
[88] *War of the Rebellion: Official Records of the Union and Confederate Armies*, U.S. Government Printing Office, 1891

bales. A very large number of cotton gins and presses were also destroyed. (H. W. Slocum)[89]

Macon & Western (Macon, Savannah)

The Macon and Western came to be in December 1845, when a group of investors linked to the Georgia RR took over a moribund railroad named the Monroe RR & Banking Co. Although the railroad never went anywhere the the west, its name reflected future hopes that were never realized.

By 1838, the Monroe RR was complete from Macon to Forsyth, Georgia, with an extension to Griffith in 1842. On September 4, 1846, the Macon and Western was completed into Atlanta (East Point).

The M&W, too, was part of the four spokes of railroads that connected Atlanta to the outside world. Sherman made attempts to destroy the railroad via cavalry in July and August 1864, such as this attack on Lovejoy's Station by Edward McCook:

> He then pushed for the railroad, reaching it at Lovejoy's Station at the time appointed. He burned the depot, tore up a section of the railroad [Macon & Western], five miles of telegraph wire destroyed and McCook continued to work until forced to leave off to defend himself against an accumulating force of the enemy.[90]
> (William Tecumseh Sherman, *Official Record*)

Major R. Root, 8th Iowa, described the damage done in Lovejoy's Station:

> At Lovejoy's Station a detachment of the Eighth Iowa burned part of a train loaded with government stores, consisting of tobacco, lard, and arms. The tobacco was estimated by the citizens to be

---

[89] *War of the Rebellion: Official Records of the Union and Confederate Armies*, U.S. Government Printing Office, 1891
[90] *War of the Rebellion: Official Records of the Union and Confederate Armies*, U.S. Government Printing Office, 1891

worth $120,000. The depot, water-tank, and road was destroyed for two miles by my command.[91] (*Official Record*)

However, McCook's raid, which was interrupted by the arrival of Joe Wheeler's cavalry, only interfered with operations for a few days.

Another attempt to destroy the M&W RR link with Atlanta would occur with a cavalry raid by Judson Kilpatrick during the third week of August 1864:

> I suspended the execution of my orders for the time being and ordered General Kilpatrick to make up a well appointed force of about 5,000 cavalry, and to move from his camp about Sandtown during the night of the 18th to the West Point road and break it good near Fairburn, then to proceed across to the Macon road and tear it up thoroughly, but to avoid as far as possible the enemy's infantry, but to attack any cavalry he could find. I thought this cavalry would save the necessity of moving the main army across, and that in case of his success it would leave me in better position to take full advantage of the result. General Kilpatrick got off at the time appointed and broke the West Point road and afterward reached the Macon road at Jonesborough, where he whipped Ross' cavalry and got possession of the railroad, which he held for five hours, damaging it considerably, but a brigade of the enemy's infantry, which had been dispatched below Jonesborough in cars, was run back and disembarked, and with Jackson's rebel cavalry made it impossible for him to continue his work. He drew off to the east and made a circuit and struck the railroad about Lovejoy's Station, but was again threatened by the enemy, who moved on shorter lines, when he charged through their cavalry, taking many prisoners, of which he brought in 70, and captured a 4-gun battery, which he destroyed, except one gun, which he brought in. He estimated the damage done to the road as enough to interrupt its use for ten days, after which he returned by a circuit north and east, reaching Decatur on the 22d.

---

[91] *War of the Rebellion: Official Records of the Union and Confederate Armies*, U.S. Government Printing Office, 1891

> After an interview with General Kilpatrick I was satisfied that whatever damage he had done would not produce the result desired, and I renewed my orders for the movement of the whole army. This involved the necessity of raising the siege of Atlanta, taking the field with our main force and using it against the communications of Atlanta instead of against its intrenchments.[92]
> (William Tecumseh Sherman, *Official Record*)

The final breaking of the link occurred with the Battle of Jonesboro August 31 - September 1, 1864.

In 1872, the M&W was bought by the Central Railroad.

Atlanta & West Point (Montgomery)

Construction on what would become the Atlanta and West Point Railroad[93] began in the Fall of 1849. Since the planned southwestern terminus was to be West Point, the northeastern terminus was named East Point, as it is still named today. In early 1854, the railroad reached La Grange, and in May 1854, it reached West Point, and linked up with the Montgomery and West Point Railroad. However, the A&L RR and the M&WP RR had different gauges – the latter using 4'8.5", and the former using 5 feet.

On December 22, 1857, the Atlanta and La Grange Railroad official changed its name to the Atlanta and West Point Railroad.

The A&WP RR sustained damage during McCook's raid on July 28, 1864, in both Palmetto and Fairburn. At around 6:00 on that date, McCook burned the depot at Palmetto, and destroyed "Two and one-half miles of the Atlanta and West Point Railroad and telegraph wire". Also, "a few box cars containing a quantity of salt, bacon, flour, and other

---
[92] *War of the Rebellion: A Compilation of the Official Records of the Union and Confederate Armies, The* (Government Printing Office, 1897)
[93] Atlanta and La Grange RR at the time

commissary stores" were destroyed. The "glare of the light" could be seen in Newnan, to the south:

> Last Thursday, the 28th, about dark, scouts brought in word that the enemy was crossing the river in large force. There was little heed paid to the report, as we had heard so many lately. About 9 o'clock the whole sky was illuminated by a glare of light, in the direction of Palmetto, a small town on the railroad. We knew then what we had to expect, and got ready as usual; whiskey, and every thing of any consequence, was sent off; the men who were able taking to the woods.[94]

Like the Macon & Western RR, the A&WP RR also sustained damage during Kilpatrick's raid in August 1864. See the M&W RR section above for more details.

The Battle of Brown's Mill began near the site of the A&WP RR depot in Newnan, GA

Central Railroad

The building of the Central Railroad began in early 1838, when 26 miles of track had been laid from Savannah to Eden. 45 more miles of grading had also been done, to Guyton. By May

---
[94] *A Journal of Hospital Life in the Confederate Army of Tennessee*, by Kate Cumming (John P. Morton & Co., 1866)

1839, track was complete to Millen (78 miles from Savannah), and grading to Sandersville (133 miles from Savannah). By 1841, the line was complete from Savannah to Tennille. In October 1843, track was completed to Macon.

1851 Central Railroad and Macon & Western Railroad schedules[95]

---

[95] From *American Railways Guide for the United States* (Curran Dinsmore, April 1851)

If the names of some of these towns – Savannah, Millen, Sandersville, Tennille and Macon – sound familiar from Sherman's March to the Sea, you can get a pretty good idea what one of the main targets of Sherman's March was – the destruction of the Central RR. Some examples of the destruction wrought follow.

<u>Macon</u>

General Kilpatrick waited at Clinton until the arrival of the head of the infantry column, at 12 m., when he moved out toward Macon on the left Macon road. He met the enemy's cavalry about four miles from Macon, drove them in, and charged their works, defended by infantry and artillery. The head of his column got inside the works, but could not hold them. He succeeded in reaching the railroad and destroyed about one mile of the track. The road was struck in two or three places by the cavalry, besides the above, and a train of cars burned. (O. O. Howard, Major-General)[96]

<u>Griswoldville</u>

A detachment of Ninth Michigan Cavalry, Captain Ladd commanding, had already struck the railroad at Griswold Station, capturing a train of thirteen cars, loaded with engine driving wheels and springs for same. The station was destroyed; pistol, soap and candle factories burned. (J. Kilpatrick, Brigadier-General, Commanding Cavalry). [97]

CENTRAL RAILROAD COMPANY, Savannah, November 21, 1864.

Major - General McLAWS:

...I received the following from Augusta, from our operator at Gordon, written yesterday:

---

[96] *War of the Rebellion: Official Records of the Union and Confederate Armies*, U.S. Government Printing Office, 1891

[97] *War of the Rebellion: Official Records of the Union and Confederate Armies*, U.S. Government Printing Office, 1891

The lumber train was captured at Griswoldville and burned today. Negroes all safe. Destroyed the machine shops and foundry and Georgia Chemical Works. Road burned at Griswoldville.

Very respectfully, your obedient servant,

R. R. CUYLER, President.[98]

Tennille

...my command marched to the Georgia Central Railroad at Tennille Station and destroyed six miles of track, the railroad depot, Government warehouses, and 324 bales of cotton... (Brigadier-General N. J. Jackson)[99]

Milledgeville

Large quantities of arms, ammunition, and accouterments were found and destroyed , as well as salt and other public property... The railroad depot, two arsenals, a powder magazine, and other public buildings and shops, were burned. The railroad track for five miles toward Gordon was destroyed. (A. S. Williams, Brigadier-General)[100]

Millen

General Kilpatrick has returned to Louisville. He destroyed portions of the road between Millen and Augusta, and had some severe fighting with Wheeler.[101] (H. W. Slocum)

Waynesboro

Struck the railroad at Waynesborough...having destroyed the station and train of cars captured day previous, and partly burned the bridge over Brier Creek. Here I learned that our prisoners had

---

[98] *War of the Rebellion: Official Records of the Union and Confederate Armies*, U.S. Government Printing Office, 1891
[99] *War of the Rebellion: Official Records of the Union and Confederate Armies*, U.S. Government Printing Office, 1891
[100] *War of the Rebellion: Official Records of the Union and Confederate Armies*, U.S. Government Printing Office, 1891
[101] *War of the Rebellion: Official Records of the Union and Confederate Armies*, U.S. Government Printing Office, 1891

been moved from Millen, Ga.; and, after destroying track sufficient to prevent transportation for a few days, deemed it prudent to retire our infantry in direction of Louisville, Ga.[102] (Brigadier General Judson Kilpatrick)

We burned the bridge, about 120 feet long, over Brier Creek, four miles north of Waynesborough, during Saturday night. Captured at Waynesborough a train of 8 box and 3 platform cars and a locomotive, all of which were burned, the cargo, hogs for Augusta, turned loose. (Jos. C. Audenried, Captain, U. S. Army)[103]

"Central of Georgia Railroad, Passenger Station & Train Shed" in Savannah, GA[104]

Although the Central Railroad had been almost totally destroyed by Sherman in 1864, by 1869, is was substantially functional again.

---

[102] *War of the Rebellion: Official Records of the Union and Confederate Armies*, U.S. Government Printing Office, 1891
[103] *War of the Rebellion: Official Records of the Union and Confederate Armies*, U.S. Government Printing Office, 1891
[104] Library of Cong. http://www.loc.gov/pictures/item/ga0837.photos.055871p/

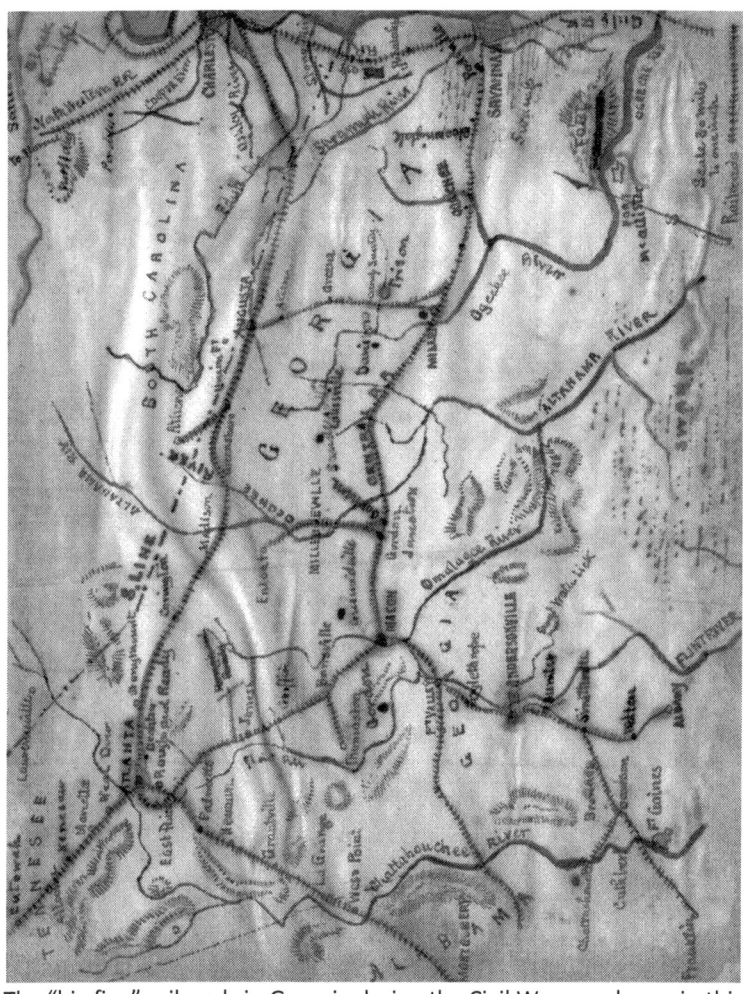

The "big five" railroads in Georgia during the Civil War are shown in this map made between 1861/65[105]

---

[105] Library of Congress http://hdl.loc.gov/loc.ndlpcoop/gvhs01.vhs00053

Sites Associated with Georgia Civil War Railroads	Address or Location
1849 Tunnel Hill W&A Depot (next to the Visitor's Center)	215 Clisby Austin Road, Tunnel Hill, GA
1849 W&A Depot (Adairsville)	101 Public Square, Adairsville Georgia 30103
1849 W&A Depot (Dalton)	110 Depot Street, Dalton, 30720
1849 W&A Depot (Ringgold)	155 Depot Street, Ringgold, Georgia 30736
A&WP RR depot (site of the beginning of the Battle of Brown's Mill)	60 East Broad Street, Newnan, GA
Allatoona Pass (W&A)	Old Allatoona Road, Emerson, GA
Central of Georgia Railroad: Savannah Shops and Terminal Facilities	W. Broad and Liberty Sts., Savannah, Georgia
Georgia State Railroad Museum	655 Louisville Rd., Savannah, GA 31401
Southern Museum (home of the W&A locomotive *General*)	2628 Cherokee Street, Kennesaw, GA 30144

Cemeteries

The idea of national cemeteries for Union dead was in full swing by July 17, 1862, when Congress granted the power to President Abraham Lincoln "to purchase cemetery grounds and cause them to be securely enclosed, to be used as a national cemetery for the soldiers who shall die in the service of the country." By the end of 1862, 14 national cemeteries had been established.

By February 1864, Union soldiers were being interred in the cemetery at Andersonville. It was declared a National Cemetery on June 26, 1865.

Marietta National Cemetery was established in 1866 by General George Thomas, primarily to house Union soldiers killed during the Atlanta Campaign.[106]

As a general rule, the only Confederate soldiers buried in National Cemeteries were those that died in Union hospitals during the War. One exception is Confederate Major General Joseph Wheeler who is interred in Arlington National Cemetery because of his service during the Spanish-American War, and the Philippine Insurrection.

Confederate cemeteries throughout Georgia are generally a much more localized affair, often started by local women's or veteran's groups in the towns within which they reside. They range in size from a handful of interments, to many hundreds. In modern times, the graves are often maintained by members of local Sons of Confederate Veterans or United Daughters of the Confederacy.

---

[106] http://www.cem.va.gov/cem/docs/factsheets/history.pdf

The following list is not exhaustive, but it is reasonably complete.

Cemetery	Address or Location
Andersonville National Cemetery	760 POW Road, Andersonville, GA 31711
Blackwell Cemetery	E. Piedmont Road near Bob Bettis Road, Marietta, GA
Cassville Confederate Cemetery	Cassville-White & Shinall Gaines Roads, Cassville, GA
Confederate Cemetery	Miller St. near Douglas St., Lagrange, GA
Confederate Cemetery and Monument	West Cuyler Street and Lynn St., Dalton, GA
Covington Confederate Cemetery	Conyers and Davis Sts., Covington, GA
Evergreen Cemetery	3655 Atlanta Highway, Athens, GA 30606
Forsyth Confederate Cemetery	S. Harris St. and Newton Memorial Drive, Forsyth, GA
Fort Tyler Cemetery	US 29 and E. 12th St., West Point, GA
Glenwood Cemetery	S. Hightower St., Thomaston, GA
Greenwood Cemetery	Adams and Lamar Sts., Barnesville, GA
Greenwood Cemetery	Hamilton Ave., Cuthbert, GA
Guyton City Cemetery	Cemetery Rd., Guyton, GA
Kingston Confederate Cemetery	Johnson and Cemetery Streets, Kingston, GA
Laurel Grove Cemetery	Ogeechee Road and Kollock Street, Savannah, Georgia

Cemetery	Address or Location
Laurel Hill Cemetery	600-700 East Jackson Street (U. S. Hwy. 319 N.), Thomasville, GA 31792
Linwood Cemetery	621 Linwood Blvd, Columbus, GA 31901
Madison Cemetery	E. Central Avenue, Madison, GA
Magnolia Cemetery	702 3rd Street Augusta, GA 30901
Marietta Confederate Cemetery	Cemetery and W. Atlanta Streets, Marietta, GA
Marietta National Cemetery	500 Washington Ave NE, Marietta, GA 30060
Memory Hill Cemetery	300 W. Franklin St., Milledgeville, GA
Milner Confederate Cemetery	140 Lawrence Rd, Milner, GA
Myrtle Hill Cemetery	Branham Ave. at South Broad St., Rome, GA 30161
New Armuchee Cemetery	U.S 27 and Scenic Road, Armuchee, GA (north of Rome, where U.S. 27 crosses Armuchee Creek)
New Hope Church	31 Bobo Road, Dallas, GA 30132
New Park Cemetery	Hartford Road, Fort Gaines, GA
Oak Grove Cemetery	East Church and Reese Streets, Americus, GA
Oak Hill Cemetery	96 Jefferson Street, Newnan, GA
Oak Hill Cemetery	E. Poplar Street, Griffin, GA 30223
Oak Lawn Cemetery	S. Camellia Blvd., Fort Valley, Ga
Oakland Cemetery	248 Oakland Ave SE, Atlanta,

Cemetery	Address or Location
	GA
Oxford Cemetery	100 Hamill St, Oxford, GA 30054 (Hearn Nature Trail)
Patrick R. Cleburne Memorial Cemetery	Johnson and McDonough Streets, Jonesboro, GA
Ramah Church	Hwy 57, Gordon, GA (south of the town)
Resaca Confederate Cemetery	Hwy 41 and Confederate Cemetery Road, Resaca, GA
Riverside Cemetery	200 Cotton Ave, Albany, GA 31701
Rose Hill Cemetery	1071 Riverside Dr, Macon, GA 31201
Sandersville City Cemetery	Between West Church Street and West Haynes Street, Sandersville, GA
Southview Cemetery	Elm Street SE and South Street SW, Covington, GA
Stonewall Cemetery	Near 797 Memorial Dr., Griffin, GA 30223
The Rock Cemetery	83 The Rock Road, Upson County, GA
Utoy Church	1465 Cahaba Drive SW, Atlanta, GA 30311
Waynesboro Cemetery	SR24 and Jones Ave., Waynesboro, GA
Westend Cemetery	W. Screven St. (US 84) at N. Laurel St., Quitman, GA
Westview Cemetery	1680 Westview Dr SW, Atlanta, GA 30310

Resaca Confederate Cemetery

300 Civil War graves at Myrtle Hill Cemetery, Rome, GA

Obelisk in the Confederate Cemetery at Cassville, GA

Lion of the South Monument at Oakland Cemetery, Atlanta, GA

Marietta Confederate Cemetery

Confederate graves in Utoy Church Cemetery, Atlanta, GA

Marietta National Cemetery

Oak Hill Cemetery, Newnan, GA

Westview Cemetery, Atlanta, GA

299 dead in the Confederate cemetery in Forsyth, GA

Patrick Cleburne Confederate Cemetery (1872)

Soldier's Cemetery at Oxford, GA

Soldier's Square at Rose Hill Cemetery, Macon, GA

Union soldiers may be buried here, in the city cemetery at Sandersville, GA

Sources

- *A Journal of Hospital Life in the Confederate Army of Tennessee*, by Kate Cumming (John P. Morton & Co., 1866)
- *A Memoir of the Life and Public Service of Joseph E. Johnston*, edited by Bradley Tyler Johnson (R. H. Woodward & Company, 1891
- *A Scriptural Examination of the Institution of Slavery in the United States*, by Howell Cobb (1856)
- *Advance and Retreat*, by John Bell Hood (G. T. Beauregard, for The Hood Orphan Memorial Publication Fund, 1880)
- *American Railways Guide for the United States* (Curran Dinsmore, April 1851)
- Appleton's Annual Cyclopedia for 1864, vol. IV
- *Campaigns of Wheeler and His Cavalry*, 1862-1865, edited By W. C. Dodson, Historian (Hudgins Publishing Company, 1899)
- *Capturing a Locomotive*, by William Pittenger (National Tribune, 1881)
- *Cornerstone Speech*, Andrew Stephens, March 21, 1861, Savannah, Georgia
- *Evening Telegraph*, The (Philadelphia, Pennsylvania, July 1, 1864)
- *From Manassas to Appomattox: Memoirs of the Civil War in America*, by James Longstreet (J. B. Lippincott Company, 1895)
- *Georgia in the War, 1861-1865*, by Charles Edgeworth Jones (1909)
- *Georgia, Historical and Industrial*, by Obediah B. Stevens and Robert F. Wright (Georgia. Dept. of Agriculture, 1901)
- *Ghost Trains & Depots of Georgia (1833-1933)*, by Les R. Winn (1995)
- *Gleanings From Southland*, by Kate Cumming (Roberts & Son, 1895)
- *Johnson, A. J., Johnson's New Illustrated (Steel Plate) Family Atlas with Descriptions, Geographical, Statistical, and Historical* (A. J. Johnson & Ward, 1862)
- *Memoirs of Gen. William T. Sherman*, by William Tecumseh Sherman (D. Appleton & Company, 1891)
- *Memoirs of General William T. Sherman, Volume 2* (Second Edition), by William Tecumseh Sherman (D. Appleton and Company, 1904)
- *Memories: A Record of Personal Experience and Adventure During Four Years of War*, by Fannie A. Beers (1888)

- National Archives and Records Administration, 533402
- *The Confederate Records of the State of Georgia, Volume 2* (Georgia Legislature, 1909)
- *The Crisis*, Speech of Hon. Robert Toombs. Delivered Before the Georgia Legislature, December 7, 1860.
- *The Evening Telegraph*, Philadelphia, Pennsylvania, July 1, 1864
- *The Sun*, New York City, December 16, 1864
- *War of the Rebellion: A Compilation of the Official Records of the Union and Confederate Armies, The* (Government Printing Office, 1897)

All modern photos by Robert C. Jones, unless otherwise noted

Links

http://chroniclingamerica.loc.gov/
http://teachingamericanhistory.org/library/index.asp?documentprint=76
http://www.cem.va.gov/cem/docs/factsheets/history.pdf
http://www.civilwartraveler.com/WEST/GA/more-georgia.html
http://www.gastateparks.org/core/item/page.aspx?s=153653.0.1.5
http://www.georgiaencyclopedia.org/articles/history-archaeology/civil-war-industry-and-manufacturing
http://www.gutenberg.org/files/4361/4361-h/4361-h.htm#ch19
http://www.nps.gov/history/nr/travel/Augusta/sibleymill.html
http://www.sonofthesouth.net/union-generals/sherman/memoirs/general-sherman-march-sea.htm
Library of Congress http://www.loc.gov/pictures/item/00652519/
Library of Congress http://www.loc.gov/pictures/item/2005681127/
Library of Congress http://www.loc.gov/pictures/item/cwp2003000446/PP/
Library of Congress http://hdl.loc.gov/loc.gmd/g3701p.cw0014000
Library of Congress http://hdl.loc.gov/loc.gmd/g3866sm.gcw0102000
Library of Congress http://hdl.loc.gov/loc.gmd/g3924k.cw0149000
Library of Congress http://hdl.loc.gov/loc.ndlpcoop/gvhs01.vhs00053
Library of Congress http://hdl.loc.gov/loc.ndlpcoop/gvhs01.vhs00054
Library of Congress http://hdl.loc.gov/loc.ndlpcoop/gvhs01.vhs00179
Library of Congress http://hdl.loc.gov/loc.ndlpcoop/gvhs01.vhs00304
Library of Congress http://www.loc.gov/pictures/item/2003662987/
Library of Congress http://www.loc.gov/pictures/item/2004660818/
Library of Congress http://www.loc.gov/pictures/item/2004661237/
Library of Congress http://www.loc.gov/pictures/item/2006687471/
Library of Congress http://www.loc.gov/pictures/item/2011630674/
Library of Congress http://www.loc.gov/pictures/item/2011648012/
Library of Congress http://www.loc.gov/pictures/item/2012648417/
Library of Congress http://www.loc.gov/pictures/item/91481351/
Library of Congress http://www.loc.gov/pictures/item/91482113/
Library of Congress http://www.loc.gov/pictures/item/99614054/

Library of Congress http://www.loc.gov/pictures/item/brh2003000349/PP/
Library of Congress http://www.loc.gov/pictures/item/cwp2003000766/PP
Library of Congress http://www.loc.gov/pictures/item/cwp2003001167/PP/
Library of Congress http://www.loc.gov/pictures/item/cwp2003001868/PP/
Library of Congress http://www.loc.gov/pictures/item/cwp2003003004/PP/
Library of Congress http://www.loc.gov/pictures/item/cwp2003003502/PP/
Library of Congress http://www.loc.gov/pictures/item/cwp2003005420/PP/
Library of Congress http://www.loc.gov/pictures/item/cwp2003005431/PP/
Library of Congress http://www.loc.gov/pictures/item/det1994013530/PP/
Library of Congress http://www.loc.gov/pictures/item/ga0837.photos.055871p/
Library of Congress http://hdl.loc.gov/loc.gmd/g3921s.cws00028
Library of Congress http://www.loc.gov/pictures/item/00652832
Library of Congress http://www.loc.gov/pictures/item/2003663826
Library of Congress http://www.loc.gov/pictures/item/2003679761
Library of Congress http://www.loc.gov/pictures/item/2004660836
Library of Congress http://www.loc.gov/pictures/item/91482104
Library of Congress http://www.loc.gov/pictures/item/91482215
Library of Congress http://www.loc.gov/pictures/item/cwp2003000359/PP
Library of Congress http://www.loc.gov/pictures/item/cwp2003000887/PP
Library of Congress http://www.loc.gov/pictures/item/ggb2006005343
www.wikimedia.org
www.wikipedia.org

Front Cover: Map of Andersonville
Library of Congress http://hdl.loc.gov/loc.ndlpcoop/gvhs01.vhs00179;
Modern photo of Fort Pulaski

Appendix One – Battles in Georgia

from *Georgia in the War, 1861-1865*[107]

Acworth, Oct. 4, 1864
Alexander's Bridge, Sept. 18, 1863
Allatoona, Oct. 5, 1864
Alpine, Sept. 3, 5, 8, 12, 1863; May —, 1864
Armuchee Creek, May 15, 1864.
Atlanta, July 22, 23, Aug. 25, Sept. 2, Nov. 6, 9, 1864
Bear Creek Station, Nov. 16, 1864
Beaulieu, Fort, Dec. 14-21, 1864
Atlanta Campaign, May 1-Sept. 8, 1864
Atlanta & West Point R. R., July 27-31, 1864
Augusta Arsenal, Jan. 24, 1861
Bald Hill, July 21, 1864
Ball's Ferry, Nov. 23-25, 1864
Barnesville, April 19, 1865
Big Shanty, June 9, Oct. 3, 1864
Blue Bird Gap, Sept. 11, 1863
Brunswick, June 8, 1863
Brush Mountain, June —, 1864
Bryan Court House, Dec. 8, 1864
Buck Creek, Dec. 7, 1864
Buck Head, July 18, 1864
Buck Head Church, Nov. 28, 1864
Buck Head Creek, Nov. 28, Dec. 2, 1864
Buck Head Station, Nov. 19, 1864
Burke's Mill, Feb. 18-19, 1864
Burnt Hickory, May 24, 1864
Buzzard Roost, Feb. 24-25, 1864; April 23, 1865
Buzzard Roost Gap, May 8-11, Oct. 13-14, 1864
Calhoun, May 16, June 10, 1864
Campbellton, July 28, Sept. 10, 1864
Camp Creek, Aug. 18, Sept. 30, 1864
Cartersville, May 20, July 24, Sept. 20, 1864.
Cassville, May 18-19, 24, 1864
Catlett's Gap, Sept. 15-18, 1863
Catoosa Platform, Feb. 27, 1864
Catoosa Springs, May 3, 1864
Catoosa Station, Feb. 23, 1864

---

[107] *Georgia in the War, 1861-1865*, by Charles Edgeworth Jones (1909)

Cave Spring Road, Oct. 13, 1864
Chattahoochee Railroad Bridge, Aug. 26-Sept. 1, 1864
Chattahoochee River, July 5-17, 1864
Chattooga River, Sept. 12, 1863
Cheney's Farm, June 22-27, 1864
Chickamauga, Sept. 19-20, 1863.
Chickamauga Campaign, Aug. 16-Sept. 22, 1863
Chickamauga Creek, Jan. 30, May 3, 1864
Clear Creek, July 30, 1864
Clinton, July 30, Nov. 20, 21-23, 1864
Columbus, April 16, 17, 1865
Coosaville Road, Oct. 12-13, 1864
Coosawattee River, April 1-4, 1865
Cotton River Bridge, Nov. 16, 1864
Covington, July 22-24, 1864
Crow's Valley, Feb. 24-25, 1864
Cuyler's Plantation, Dec. 9, 1864
Cypress Swamp, Dec. 7, 1864
Dallas, May 24, 26-June 1, Oct. 7, 1864
Dallas Line, May 25-June 5, 1864
Dalton, Jan. 6, 21-23, Feb. 22-27, May 13, Aug. 14, Oct. 13, Nov. 30, Dec. 5, 1864; March 13, 14, 1865
Darien, June 11, Sept. 22, 1863
Davisboro, Nov. 28, 1864
Davis Cross Roads, Sept. 11, 1863
Davis House, Sept. 11, 1863
Dedmon's Trace, April 10, 1864
Deer Head Cove, March 29-31, 1864
Dirt Town, Sept. 12, 1863
Doboy River, Nov. 13-18, 1862
Double Bridges, April 18, 1865
Dry Valley, Sept. 21, 1863
Ducktown Road, April 3, 1864
Dug Gap, Sept. 11, 1863; May 8-11, 1864
Dyer's Ford, Sept. 18, 1863
East Macon, Nov. 20, 1864
East Point, Aug. 30, Nov. 15, 1864
East Tennessee and Georgia Railroad, Nov. 24-27, 1863
Eatonton, Nov. 21, 1864
Ebenezer Creek, Dec. 8, 1864
Eden Station, Dec. 9, 1864
Elba Island, March 7-11, 1862
Ellidge's Mill, Feb. 18-19, 1864

Etowah River, May 20, 1864
Ezra Church, July 28, 1864
Fairburn, Aug. 15, Oct. 2, 1864
Flat Creek, Oct. 11-14, 1864
Flat Rock Bridge, July 28, 1864
Flat Rock Road, Oct. 2, 1864
Flint River, Aug. 19, 1864; April 18, 1865
Flint River Bridge, Aug. 30, 1864
Floyd's Spring, May 16, 1864
Frick's Gap, Feb. 25, 26, 1864
Georgetown, April 17-30, 1865
Georgia, Jan. 3-26, 1861; Nov. 14-Dec. 31, 1864
Georgia, Central, Jan. 1-June 30, 1865
Georgia, Northern, April 7-12, May 3, 1862; Aug. 11-Oct. 19, Oct. 20-Dec. 31, 1863; Jan. 1-April 30, May 1-Nov. 13, 1864; Nov. 14, 1864; Jan. 23, 1865; Jan. 1-June 30, 1865
Georgia, Southern, Jan. 1-June 30, 1865
Georgia Central Railroad Bridge, Nov. —, 1864
Georgia Central Railroad Station No. 5, Dec. 4, 1864
Georgia Coast, Aug. 21, 1861-April 11, 1862; April 12, 1862; June 11, 1863; June 12-Dec. 31, 1863; Jan. 1-Nov. 13, 1864
Gilgal Church, June 10-July 3, 1864
Gordon, Nov. 21, 1864
Graysville, Sept. 10, Nov. 26, 1863
Griswoldville, Nov. 20-22, 1864
Hillsboro, July 30-31, 1864.
Hinesville, Dec. 16, 1864
Holly Creek, March 1, 1865
Howell's Ferry, July 5, Oct. 19, 1864
Hudson Place Salt Works, Sept. 22, 1863
Huntsville, May 24, 1864
Isham's Ford, July —, 1864
Jackson, Fort, Jan. 26, 1861; Dec. 21, 1864
Jasper, Aug. 14-15, 1864
Jenks' Bridge, Dec. 7, 1864
Johnson's Crook, Feb. 10, 1865
Jonesboro, Aug. 19, 31-Sept. 1, Nov. 15, 1864
Jug Tavern, Aug. 3, 1864
Kennesaw Mountain, June 19-25, 1864; June 27, 1864
Kennesaw Water Tank, Oct. 3, 1864
Kingston, May 18-19, Nov. 10-11, 1864
Kolb's Farm, June 22, 1864

LaFayette, Sept. 10, 18, 14, Dec. 12, 14, 21-23, 1863; April 11-13, 24-25, June 24, Oct. 12, 1864
LaFayette Road, Sept. 12, 1863
Lawrenceville, Oct. 27, 1864
Lay's Ferry, May 15, 1864
Lee and Gordon's Mills, Sept. 11-13, 16-18, 1863
Lee's Cross Roads, May 2, 1864
Leet's Tan Yard, Sept. 12, 1863; March 5, 1864
Leggett's Hill, July 21, 1864
Lithonia, July 28, 1864
Little Ogeechee River, Dec. 4, 5, 1864
Lookout Church, Sept. 21, 1863
Lookout Creek, May 3, 1862
Lookout Mountain, Sept. 9, 1863
Lost Mountain, June —, Oct. 4-7, 1864
Louisville, Nov. 29, 30, 1864
Lovejoy's Station, July 29, Aug. 18-22, Sept. 2-5, Nov. 16, 1864
Lumpkin County, Sept. 15, 1864
Lumpkin's Station, Dec. 4, 1864
McAfee's Cross Roads, June 11, 1864
McAllister, Fort, June 29, 1862; Jan. 27, Feb. 28, March 9, 1863; Feb. 1, March 3 (1864?), Dec. 13, 1864
McDonough Road, Oct. 2, Nov. 6, 1864
Mcintosh County, Aug. 2-4, 1864
McLemore's Cove, Sept. 11, 1863; March 30-April 1, 1864; Feb. 1, 1865
Macon & Western Railroad, July 27-31, 1864
Marietta, June 10-July 3, 1864
Mill Creek Gap, May 8-11, 1864
Milledgeville, Nov. 23, 1864
Millen's Grove, Dec. 1, 1864
Mimm's Mills, April 20, 1865
Monteith Swamp, Dec. 9, 1864
Moon's Station, Oct. 4, 1864
Mulberry Creek, Aug. 3, 1864
Neal Dow Station, July 4, 1864
New Hope Church, May 25-June 5, Oct. 5, 1864
Nickajack Creek, June —, 1864
Nickajack Gap, March 9, May 7, 1864
Nickajack Trace, April 23, 1864
Noonday Creek, June —, 1864
Northern Georgia, Sept. 29-Nov. 13, 1864
Noyes' Creek, June —, Oct. 2-3, 1864
Oconee River, Nov. 23-25, 1864

Ogeechee Canal, Dec. 9, 1864
Ogeechee River, Dec. 7, 1864
Oglethorpe Barracks, Jan. 26, 1861
Olley's Creek, June —, 1864
Ossabaw Island, July 3, 1863
Ossabaw Sound, June 3, 1864
Owens' Ford, Sept. 17, 1863
Pace's Ferry, July 5-17, Aug. 26, 1864
Parker's Cross Roads, May 16, 1864
Peachtree Creek, July 19, 20, 1864
Pea Vine Creek, Sept. 10, 1863
Pea Vine Ridge, Sept. 18, 1863
Pickens County, July —, 1864
Pickett's Mills, May 25-June 5, 1864
Pigeon Mountain, Sept. 15-18, 1863
Pine Hill, June 6-18 (?), 1864
Pine Log Creek, May 18, 1864
Pleasant Hill, April 18, 1865
Pooler Station, Dec. 9, 1864
Powder Springs, June —, Oct. 2-3, 1864
Pulaski, Fort, Jan. 3, 1861; April 10-11, 1862
Pumpkin Vine Creek, May 25-June 5, 1864
Red Oak, Aug. 19, 29, 1864
Reed's Bridge, Sept. 18, 1863
Resaca, May 14, 1864
Reynolds' Plantation, Nov. 28, 1864
Ringgold, Sept. 11, 17, Dec. 5, 13, 1863; Feb. 8, 18, April 27 1864; March 20, 1865
Ringgold Gap, Nov. 27, 1863; May 2, 1864
Rock Spring, Sept. 12, 1863
Rocky Creek Bridge, April 20, 1865
Rocky Creek Church, Dec. 2, 1864
Rocky Face Ridge, Feb. 24-25, May 8-11, 1864
Rome, April 26-May 3, Sept. 10, 11, 1863; Jan. 25-Feb, 5, May 15, 17, July 11-13, 28-29, Aug. 11-15, Oct. 10-13, 1864
Rome Cross Roads, May 16, 1864
Rosedew, Fort, Dec. 14-21, 1864
Rossville, Sept. 11, 17, 21, Dec. 5, 14, 1863
Roswell, Sept. 26, 1864
Rottenwood Creek, July 4, 1864
Rough and Ready, Nov. 15, 1864
Rough and Ready Station, Aug. 31, 1864
Ruff's Mill, July 4, 1864

Ruff's Station, Oct. 19, 1864
Salt Springs, Oct. 1, 1864
Sandersville, Nov. 25, 26, 1864
Sand Mountain, Oct. 2, 1864
Sandtown, Aug. 15, 1864
Savannah, Dec. 10, 11-21, 1864
Savannah Campaign, Nov. 15-Dec. 21, 1864
Savannah River, March 7-11, Sept. 30-Oct. 3, 1862
Shadna Church, Oct. 2, 1864
Shady Grove, Dec. 1, 1864
Ship's Gap, Oct. 16, 1864
Sisters Ferry, Dec. 7, 1864
Snake Creek Gap, May 8, Sept. 15, Oct. 15, 1864
Snapflnger Creek, July 27, 1864
South Newport, Aug. 17, 1864
South River, July 27-31, Oct. 24, 1864
Spaulding's, Nov. 7, 1862
Spring Creek, Sept. 18, 1863
Springfield, Dec. 10, 1864
Spring Hill, April 20, 1865
Spring Place, Feb. 27, April 1-4, 1865
Statesboro, Dec. 4, 1864
Station No. 5, Georgia Central Railroad, Dec. 4, 1864
Stevens' Gap, Sept. 6, 18, 1863; Feb. 25-26, 1864
Stilesboro, May 23, June 9, 1864
Stockbridge, Nov. 15, 1864
Stone Church, Feb. 7, May 1, 1864
Subligna, Jan. 22, 1864
Sugar Valley, May 8-13, 1864
Sulphur Springs, Sept. 2-5, 1864
Summervllle, Sept. 6-7, 10, 13, 15, 1863; May —, Oct. 18, 1864; May 5, 1865.
Sweet Water Creek, Oct. 2-3, 1864
Sylvan Grove, Nov. 27, 1864
Taylor's Ridge, Nov. 27, 1863; April 14, 27, 1864
Thomas' Station, Dec. 3, 1864
Tifton, May 13, Oct. 13, 1864
Tobesofkee Creek, April 20, 1865
Towaliga Bridge, Nov. 17, 1864
Trenton, Aug. 28-31, Nov. 18, 1863
Trickum's Cross Roads, Oct. 26-29, 1864
Trion Factory, Sept. 15, 1863

Tunnel Hill, Sept. 11, 1863; Feb. 23, 24, April 29, May 2, 6-7 1864; March 3, 1865
Turner's Ferry, July 5-17, Aug. 26, Oct. 19, 1864
Tybee Island, Nov. 24, 1861
Tyler, Fort, April 16, 1865
Utoy Creek, Aug. 6, 1864
Van Wert, Oct. 9-10, 1864
Varnell's Station, May 7, 9, 12, 1864
Varnell's Station Road, May 4, 1864
Venus Point, Feb. 15, 1862
Vernon River, Dec. 15-21, 1864
Walnut Creek, Nov. 20, 1864
Warsaw Sound, June 17, 1863
Watkins' Ferry, May 3, 1862
Waynesboro, Nov. 27-28, Dec. 4, 1864
Westbrook's, Oct. 2, 1864
West Point, April 16, 1865
Whitemarsh Island, March 30-31, April 16, 1862; Feb. 22, 1864
Wilmington Island, March 30-31, 1862
Wilmington Narrows, Jan. 26-28, 1862

Appendix Two - General Officers Of The Confederate Army Appointed From Georgia

Table compiled from *Georgia in the War, 1861-1865*[108]

Name	Highest Rank	Date of Rank
Edward Porter Alexander	Brigadier-General of artillery, P.A.C.S.[109]	February 26, 1864
George Thomas Anderson	Brigadier-General	November 1, 1862
Robt. H. Anderson	Brigadier-General, P.A.C.S.	July 26, 1864
Henry Lewis Benning	Brigadier-General	January 17, 1863
William R. Boggs	Brigadier-General	November 4, 1862
William M. Browne	Brigadier-General	February 18, 1865
Goode Bryan	Brigadier-General	August 29, 1863
Howell Cobb	Major-General	September 9, 1863
Thomas R. R. Cobb	Brigadier-General	November 1, 1862
Alfred Holt Colquitt	Brigadier-General	September 1, 1862
Philip Cook	Brigadier-General	August 5, 1864
Alfred Cumming	Brigadier-General	October 29, 1862
George Doles	Brigadier-General	November 1, 1862
Dudley McIver DuBose	Brigadier-General	November 16, 1864
Clement A. Evans	Brigadier-General	May 19, 1864
William Montgomery Gardner	Brigadier-General	November 14, 1861

---

[108] *Georgia in the War, 1861-1865*, by Charles Edgeworth Jones (1909)
[109] Provisional Army of the Confederate States

Name	Highest Rank	Date of Rank
Lucius J. Gartrell	Brigadier-General	August 22, 1864
Victor J. B. Girardey	Brigadier-General	July 30, 1864
John Brown Gordon	Major-General, P. A. C. S.	May 14, 1864
William J. Hardee	Lieutenant-General	October 10, 1862
George Paul Harrison, Jr.	A Colonel commanding a Brigade	
Alfred Iverson	Brigadier-General	November 1, 1862
Henry Rootes Jackson	Brigadier-General	June 4, 1861
John King Jackson	Brigadier-General	Jan. 14, 1862
David Rumple Jones	Major-General	October 11, 1862
Alexander Robert Lawton	Brigadier-General, P. A. C. S.	April 13, 1861
Fayette McLaws	Major-General	May 23, 1862
Hugh Weedon Mercer	Brigadier-General	October 29, 1861
Paul J. Semmes	Brigadier-General	March 11, 1862
James P. Simms	Brigadier-General	Dec. 8, 1864
William Duncan Smith	Brigadier-General	March 7, 1862
G. Moxley Sorrel	Brigadier-General	October 31, 1864
Isaac M. St. John	Brigadier-General and commissary-general, C. S. A.	February 16, 1865
Marcellus A. Stovall	Brigadier-General	January 20, 1863
Bryan Morel Thomas	Brigadier-General	August 4, 1864
Edward L. Thomas	Brigadier-General	November 1, 1862
Robert Toombs	Secretary of State, C. S.	July 19, 1861

Name	Highest Rank	Date of Rank
	A. (February 21, 1861) Brigadier-General	
David Emanuel Twiggs	Major-General P. A. C. S.	May 22, 1861
William Henry Talbot Walker	Brigadier-General	May 25, 1861
Henry C. Wayne	Brigadier-General P. A. C. S.	December 16, 1861; declined the appointment
Joseph Wheeler	Major-General	January 20, 1863
Claudius C. Wilson	Brigadier-General	November 16, 1863
William T. Wofford	Brigadier-General	January 17, 1863
Ambrose Ransom Wright	General	November 26, 1864
Gilbert J. Wright	Colonel in charge of a brigade	December 1864
Pierce Manning Butler Young	Major-General	December 30, 1864

Appendix Three - Local Designations of Georgia Troops in the Confederate Army

From *Georgia in the War, 1861-1865*[110]

Acworth Grays (Company C, 7th Georgia State Guards)
Albany Guards (Company E, 4th Georgia Infantry)
Alexander Cavalry (Company —, Local Defense Troops, Georgia)
Allapaha Guards (Company E, 29th Georgia Infantry)
Allapaha Rangers (Company —, in N. A. Carswell's Battalion, 22d Georgia State Guards)
Allen Rangers (Company —, Local Defense Troops, Georgia)
Alpharetta Infantry (Company F, 8th Georgia State Guards)
Altamaha Scouts (Company F, 25th Georgia Infantry)
Americus Volunteers (Company K, 9th Georgia Infantry)
Anderson Guards (Six Months Local Defense Troops, Georgia)
Anthony Greys (Company A, 60th Georgia Infantry)
Appling Cavalry (Six Months' Local Defense Troops, Georgia)
Arnett Rifles (Company I, 31st Georgia Infantry)
Athens Guards (Company —, 3rd Georgia Infantry)
Athens Reserve Corps (Local Defense Troops, Georgia)
Atlanta Arsenal Battery (Captain C. C. Campbell's Company, Georgia Artillery)
Atlanta Fire Company No. 1 (Company A, Atlanta Fire Battalion, Georgia)
Atlanta Greys (Company L, 1st Georgia Regulars)
Atlanta Greys (Company F, 8th Georgia Infantry)
Atlanta Press Guard (Company H, Atlanta Fire Battalion Georgia).
Atlanta Scouts (Company —, — Georgia Volunteers)
Atlanta Volunteers (Company —, — Georgia Volunteers)
Atlantic and Gulf Guards (Company A, 3d Battalion (Clinch's) Georgia Cavalry, afterward Company G, 4th Georgia (Clinch's) Cavalry)
Augusta Guards (Captain W. C. Dillon's Company, Georgia Volunteers)
Augusta Volunteer Artillery (Captain G. T. Barnes' Company Georgia Artillery)
Bailey Volunteers (Company B, 30th Georgia Infantry)
Bainbridge Independents (Company G, 1st Georgia Infantry)
Baker Fire Eaters (Company H, 6th Georgia Infantry)
Baker Volunteers (Company G, 3d Battalion, Georgia Infantry)
Baldwin Blues (Company H, 4th Georgia Infantry)

---

[110] *Georgia in the War, 1861-1865*, by Charles Edgeworth Jones (1909)

Baldwin Cavalry (Company C, Linton Stephens' Battalion, Local Defense Troops, Georgia)
Baldwin Infantry (Captain J. N. Moore's Company, Six Months Local Defense Troops, Georgia)
Baldwin Volunteers (Company F, 9th Georgia Infantry)
Banks County Guards (Company A, 2d Georgia Infantry)
Banks Rifles (Captain Hardy's Company, Georgia Volunteers)
Bartow Artillery (Originally Company A, 4th Battalion Georgia Infantry; afterward Company A, 60th Georgia Infantry; afterward Company A, 22d Battalion, Georgia Siege Artillery)
Bartow Avengers (Company K, 21st Georgia Infantry)
Bartow Avengers (Company E, 60th Georgia Infantry)
Bartow Avengers (Company B, 35th Georgia Infantry)
Bartow Home Guards (Company H, 4th Georgia Reserves)
Bartow Invincibles (Company H, 23d Georgia Infantry)
Bartow Invincibles (Company E, 30th Georgia Infantry)
Bartow Light Infantry (13th Georgia Volunteers)
Bartow Light Infantry (Company G, 26th Georgia Infantry)
Bartow Raid Repellers (Company C, 9th Battalion, Georgia State Guards)
Bartow Yankee Killers (Company A, 23d Georgia Infantry)
Battle Ground Guards (Company F, 48th Georgia Infantry)
Beauregard Rifles (Company C, 6th Georgia Infantry)
Beauregard Volunteers (Company C, 6th Georgia Infantry)
Bell Rangers (Company E, 19th Battalion, Georgia Infantry)
Beman Mounted Infantry (Company E, Linton Stephens' Battalion, Local Defense Troops, Georgia)
Ben Gilham Rangers (Company D, 9th Georgia State Guards)
Ben Hill Infantry (Company F, 21st Georgia Infantry)
Benjamin Infantry (Company E, 10th Georgia Infantry)
Ben Minor Dragoons (Company E, 2d Georgia Cavalry)
Berrien Cavalry (Company F, 11th Georgia State Guards)
Berrien County Light Infantry (Company I, 50th Georgia Infantry)
Berrien Minute Men (Company C, afterward 29th Georgia Infantry)
Berry Infantry (Company I, 29th Georgia Infantry)
Bibb Greys (Company —, 21st Georgia Infantry)
Bibb Volunteer Guards (Captain H. L Jewett's Company of the Macon Battalion, Local Defense Troops, Georgia)
Big Spring Cavalry (Captain J. M. Denman's Independent Company, Georgia Cavalry)
Big Spring Volunteers (Captain Joshua McConnell's Company, Georgia Volunteers)
Black Creek Volunteers (Company G, 25th Georgia Infantry)

Blodget Artillery (Originally Company I, 3d Georgia Infantry; afterward Captain Foster Blodget's Company, Georgia Artillery)
Blodget Volunteers (Originally Company I, 3d Georgia Infantry; afterward Captain Foster Blodget's Company, Georgia Artillery)
Blood Mountain Tigers (Company F, Colonel S. J. Smith's partisan rangers, Georgia Cavalry)
Blue Caps Cavalry (Company E, 2d Battalion, Georgia Cavalry; afterward Company C, 5th Georgia Cavalry)
Blue Cap Cavalry Troop (Company E, 2d Battalion, Georgia Cavalry, afterward Company C, 5th Georgia Cavalry)
Blue Ridge Guards (Captain N. F. Howard's Company, Georgia Volunteers)
Blue Ridge Tiger Regiment (Also called Banks' Troopers)
Brown Mounted Riflemen (4th Georgia State Guards)
Border Rangers (Company I, 5th Georgia Cavalry)
Border Rangers (Company B, 20th Georgia Infantry)
Bowdon Volunteers (Company B, Cobb's Legion, Georgia Cavalry)
Bragg Rifles (20th Georgia Infantry)
Breckinridge Cavalry (Company F, McDonald's Battalion, Local Defense Troops, Georgia)
Brooks Cavalry (Company D, 11th Georgia State Guards)
Brooks Rifles (Company C, 26th Georgia Infantry)
Brooks Rifles (Company H, 9th Georgia Infantry)
Brooks Volunteers (Company K, 50th Georgia Infantry)
Brown Guards (Company A, Linton Stephens' Battalion, Local Defense Troops, Georgia)
Brown Infantry (Company C, 1st Confederate Georgia Infantry)
Brown Light Infantry (Company C, 25th Georgia Infantry)
Brown Light Infantry (Company F, 25th Georgia Infantry)
Brown Rifles (Company F, 3d Georgia Infantry)
Brunswick Defenders (Company G, 1st Georgia Regulars)
Brunswick Riflemen (Company K, 26th Georgia Infantry)
Bryan Guards (Company D, 25th Georgia Infantry)
Bryan Independent Riflemen (Company A, 25th Georgia Infantry)
Bryan Independent Rifles (Company B, 25th Georgia Infantry)
Buena Vista Cavalry (Captain Brett's Company, Georgia Volunteers)
Buena Vista Guards (Company I, 2d Georgia Infantry)
Bullard Guards (Company D, 59th Georgia Infantry)
Bulloch Guards (Company C, 47th Georgia Infantry)
Bulloch Troop (Company C, 2d Battalion, Georgia Cavalry)
Burke Guards (3d Georgia Infantry)
Burke Volunteers (Company D, 48th Georgia Infantry)
Butler Van-Guard (Company G, 6th Georgia Infantry)
Butts Avengers (Company B, 7th Georgia State Guards)

Butts County Volunteers (Volunteers Company D, 6th Georgia Infantry)
Butts Invincibles (Company A, 30th Georgia Infantry)
Calhoun Cavalry (Captain W. J. Reeves' Company, Georgia State Guards).
Calhoun County Cavalry (Captain C. M. Davis' Company, T. R. Stewart's Battalion, Local Defense Troops, Georgia)
Calhoun Guards (Company D, 12th Georgia Infantry)
Calhoun Rifles (Company D, 12th Georgia Infantry)
Calhoun Repeaters (On register Company I, (L) on rolls Company H, afterward Company C, 25th Georgia Infantry)
Camden Mounted Rifles (Company C, 4th Georgia Cavalry (Clinch's)
Camden Rifles (Company B, 26th Georgia Infantry)
Campbell Greys (Company G, 30th Georgia Infantry)
Campbell Guards (Company A, 3d Battalion, Georgia Infantry; afterward Company A, 21st Georgia Infantry)
Campbell Sharpshooters (Company F, 30th Georgia Infantry)
Campbell Siege Artillery (Captain Charles G. Campbell's Company, Georgia Artillery)
Campbell Volunteers (Company E, 35th Georgia Infantry)
Canton Infantry (Company B. Cherokee Legion, Georgia Volunteers)
Carroll Cavalry (Company D, 10th Georgia State Guards)
Carroll Guards (Company I, 10th Georgia State Guards)
Carroll Infantry (Company I, 7th Georgia State Guards)
Caswell Guards (Company —, 3d Georgia Infantry)
Catoosa Infantry (Company B, 1st Battalion, Georgia Infantry)
Cave Spring (Mounted Infantry) (Company B, Floyd Legion, Georgia State Guards)
Cedartown Guards (Company D, 21st Georgia Infantry)
Central City Blues (Company H, 12th Georgia Infantry)
Centre Hill Guards (Company —, — Georgia Volunteers)
Chatham Artillery (Captain Joseph S. Claghorn's Company, Georgia Artillery; detached from 1st Georgia Volunteers)
Chatham Light Horse (Company F, 2d Battalion, Georgia Cavalry)
Chatham Siege Artillery (Companies A and B, Battalion Georgia Artillery)
Chatham Volunteers (Company E, 47th Georgia Infantry)
Chattahoochee Beauregards (Company C, 10th Georgia Infantry)
Chattahoochee Cavalry (Company —, 4th Georgia State Guards) (Blue Ridge Tiger Regiment)
Chattahoochee Defenders (Company E, 5h Georgia State Guards)
Chattahoochee Guard (Company I, 5th Georgia State Guards)
Chattahoochee Rifles (Captain H. A. Pratt's Company. Georgia - -)
Chattahoochee Volunteers (Company K, 30th Georgia Infantry)
Chattanooga Cavalry (Company G, Culberson's Battalion, Local Defense Troops, Georgia)

Chattooga Volunteers (Company —, — Georgia —)
Cherokee Brown Riflemen (Company —, — Georgia —)
Cherokee Cavalry (Company B, Phillip's Legion, Georgia Volunteers)
Cherokee Georgia Mountaineers (Company F, 28th Georgia Infantry)
Cherokee Home Guards—Infantry—(Company C, Cherokee Legion, Georgia)
Cherokee Lincoln Killers—Cavalry—(Company C, Cherokee Legion, Georgia)
Cherokee Rangers (Company F, 3d Georgia Cavalry)
Cherokee Rangers—Cavalry—(Company A, Cherokee Legion, Georgia)
Cherokee Repellers—Infantry—(Company D, Cherokee Legion, Georgia)
Cherokee Revengers—Infantry—(Company A, Cherokee Leglon, Georgia)
Cherokee Stone-Walls—Infantry—(Company G, Cherokee Legion, Georgia)
Cherokee Volunteers—Infantry—(Company E, Cherokee Legion, Georgia)
Chesatee Artillery (Captain Thomas H. Bomar's Company, Georgia Artillery; originally Company N, 38th Georgia Infantry)
Chulio Guards (Chulio Mounted Infantry) (Company F, Floyd Legion, Georgia State Guards)
Citizen Infantry (Company F, Fire Battalion, Augusta, Georgia)
City Guard (Augusta, Georgia)
City Guards (Company C, 5th Georgia State Guards)
Clarke County Guards (Company G, 9th Georgia State Guards)
Clarke County Light Artillery (Captain Franklin Roberts' Company, Arkansas Artillery; temporarily attached as Company E, 14th Battalion, Georgia Artillery)
Clay Volunteers (Captain Isham "Wood's Company, T. R. Stewart's Battalion, Local Defense Troops, Georgia)
Clay Volunteers (Company I, 51st Georgia Infantry)
Clayton Dragoons (Company F, 2d Georgia Cavalry)
Clayton Invincibles (Company I, 30th Georgia Infantry)
Clinch Cavaliers (Company G, 11th Georgia State Guards)
Clinch Rangers (—, — Georgia)
Clinch Rifles (Company A, 5th Georgia Infantry)
Clinch Volunteers (Company G, 50th Georgia Infantry)
Clinton Guards (Company B, 6th Georgia State Guards)
Coast Rifles (Company F, 1st Volunteers, Georgia Infantry)
Cobb Chattahoochee Volunteers (Company L, 7th Georgia State Guards)
Cobb Guards (Company D, 3d Georgia Reserves)
Cobb Guards (Company A. Company G, 22d Battalion, Georgia Artillery; temporarily attached)
Cobb Guards (Company B, Company H, 22d Battalion, Georgia Artillery; temporarily attached)
Cobb Invincibles (Company F, Cobb's Legion, Georgia Volunteers)
Cobb Repellers (Company K, 7th Georgia State Guards)

Cobb's Infantry (Company E, 16th Georgia Infantry)
Cobb's Legion (Georgia Volunteers)
Coffee Guards (Company C, 50th Georgia Infantry)
Coffee Revengers (Captain D. Newbern's Company, Six Months' Local Defense Troops, Georgia)
Cold Water Guards (Rebels) (Company E, 34th Georgia Infantry)
Cold Steel Guards (Company H, 49th Georgia Infantry)
Colquitt Home Guards (— Georgia Volunteers)
Colquitt Marksmen (Company H, 50th Georgia Infantry)
Columbus City Light Guard (Company A, 2d Independent Battalion, Georgia Infantry)
Columbus Guards (Company G, 2d Georgia Infantry)
Columbus Light Artillery (Captain E. Croft's Independent Company, Georgia Artillery)
Company "B" (Company D, 5th Georgia State Guards)
Confederate Continentals (Company —, O — Georgia)
Confederate Guards (Company A, 13th Georgia Infantry)
Confederate Invincibles (20th Georgia Volunteers)
Confederate Light Guards (Company G, 3d Georgia Infantry)
Confederate Sentinels (Company F, 20th Georgia Infantry)
Confederate States Sentinels (Company A, 10th Georgia Infantry)
Cotton Planters Guards (Company E, 59th Georgia Infantry)
Covington Infantry (Company I, 8th Georgia State Guards)
Cow Hunters (Also called Irwin Cow Boys,—Company A 7th Georgia Infantry)
Coweta Second District Guards (Company A, 7th Georgia Infantry)
Coweta Volunteers (Company H, 7th Georgia State Guards)
Crawford Greys (Company E, 6th Georgia Infantry)
Crawford Rangers (20th Georgia Infantry)
Crawford Rifles (Captain D. Kirkpatrick, Jr.'s Company, Georgia Volunteers)
Culpeper Hussars (Company F, Stephens' Battalion, Georgia State Guards)
Dabney Rifles (Company G, 21st Georgia Infantry)
Dade Rifles (Company K, 3d Georgia State Troops)
Dahlonega Volunteers (Company H, 1st Georgia Volunteers)
Dalton Home Guard (Company H, 1st Georgia State Guards)
Dalton Machinery Guards (Captain J. H. Bard's Company, Six Months' Local Defense Troops, Georgia)
Davis Guards (Company F, 12th Georgia Infantry)
Davis Infantry (Company K, 7th Georgia Infantry)
Davis Musketeers (Company K, 10th Georgia Infantry)
Davis Rifles (Company C, 12th Georgia Infantry)
Dawson County Independents (Company I, 22d Georgia Infantry)
Dawson Greys (Company C, 3d Georgia Infantry)

Dawson Volunteers (Company E, 5th Georgia Infantry)
Decatur Cavalry (Company I, 11th Georgia State Guards)
Decatur Grays (Company D, 17th Georgia Infantry)
Decatur Infantry (Company F, 50th Georgia Infantry)
Decatur Infantry (Captain R. Sims' Company, attached to 6th Georgia State Guards)
De Kalb Cavalry (Company A, 10th Georgia State Guards)
De Kalb Guards (Company D, 61st Georgia Infantry)
De Kalb Guards (Company B, 26th Georgia Infantry)
De Kalb Murphy Guards (Also called Murphy Guards) (Company C, afterward A, 38th Georgia Infantry)
De Kalb Silver Greys (Company B, 8th Georgia State Guards)
Delhi Rangers (Company A, 15th Georgia Infantry)
Dick Davis Guards (Company A, 9th Georgia State Guards)
Dillard Rangers (Company A, 3d Georgia Cavalry)
District Town Calvary (Captain J. Jones' Company, F. Culberson's Battalion, Local Defense Troops, Georgia)
Dixie Rangers (Company C, 65th Georgia Infantry)
Dooly Guards (Company G, 60th Georgia Infantry)
Dooly Volunteers (Captain J. D. Wilkes' Company, Wilson's Battalion, Local Defense Troops, Georgia)
Dougherty Greys (Company —, 51st Georgia Infantry)
Dougherty Guards (Company K, 51st Georgia Infantry)
Dougherty Hussars (Company D, Cobb's Legion, afterward 9th Georgia Cavalry, Georgia Volunteers)
Douglass Guards (Captain E. L Douglass's Company, Yarborough's Battalion, Local Defense Troops, Georgia)
Eagle Guards (Companies A and B, Thompson's Battalion, Local Defense Troops, Georgia)
Early Dragoons (Captain T. T. Swann's Company, Stewartt's Cavalry Battalion, Local Defense Troops, Georgia)
Early Guards (Company G, 13th Georgia Infantry)
Early Volunteers (Company A, 51st Georgia Infantry)
Echols Cavalry (Company E, 11th Georgia State Guards)
Echols Guards (Company D, 8th Georgia Infantry)
Echols Light Artillery (Captain John H. Tiller's Company, Georgia Artillery)
Effingham Hussars (Company A 2d Battalion, Georgia Cavalry)
Effingham Minute Men (Captain A. P. Longstreet's Company, Wright's Battalion. Local Defense Troops, Georgia)
Elbert Volunteers (Company H, 3d Georgia State Guards)
Emanuel Rangers (Company —, 20th Georgia Infantry)
Emmett Rifles (Originally Company C, 1st Volunteers, Georgia Infantry; afterward Company F. 22d Battalion, Georgia Siege Artillery)

Emmett Rifles (Company B, 1st Georgia Regulars)
Empire State Guards (Company I, 47th Georgia Infantry)
Etowah Invincibles (Captain Thomas M. Compton's Company, Georgia Infantry)
Evans Guards (Company K, 13th Georgia Infantry)
Factory Guards (Captain W. H. Amason's Company, Macon Battalion, Local Defense Troops, Georgia)
Fannin Guards (Company B, 4th Battalion, afterward 60th Regiment, Georgia Infantry)
Fannin Volunteers (Captain James Kincaid's Company, Gilmer Battalion, Local Defense Troops, Georgia)
Faulk Invincibles (Company E, 26th Georgia Infantry)
Fayette Grey Guards (Company I, 10th Georgia Infantry)
Fayetteville Rifle Greys (Company I, 10th Georgia Infantry)
Fayette Rangers (Company F, 13th Georgia Infantry)
Fayette Volunteers (Company H, 30th Georgia Infantry)
Firemen Guards (Captain G. S. Oberas' Company, Macon Battalion, Local Defense Troops, Georgia)
Fireside Rangers (Company C, 15th Georgia Infantry)
Flint Cavalry (Company K, 11th Georgia State Guards)
Floyd Cavalry (Company E, Floyd Legion, Georgia Volunteers)
Floyd Infantry (Company H, 8th Georgia Infantry)
Floyd Legion (Georgia Volunteers)
Floyd Rangers (Company D, Floyd Legion Georgia Volunteers)
Floyd Rifles (Company C, 2d Independent Battalion, Georgia Infantry)
Floyd Rifles (Company A, Macon Battalion, Local Defense Troops, Georgia)
Floyd Sharpshooters (Company B, 21st Georgia Infantry)
Floyd Springs Guards (Company C, 23d Georgia Infantry)
Floyd's Newton Cavalry (Company K, 10th Georgia State Guards)
Forrest's Artillery (Capt. C. O. Stillwell's Company, (I) Floyd Legion, Georgia State Troops)
Forest City Rangers (Captain C. H. Way's Company, Georgia Volunteers)
Forrest Rangers (Company H, 26th Georgia Infantry)
Forsyth Chattahoochee Cavalry (Company —, Blue Ridge Tiger Regiment, 4th Georgia State Guards)
Forsyth Mounted Greys (Company K, Cherokee Legion, Georgia Infantry)
Forsyth Mounted Guards (Company K, Cherokee Legion, Georgia Infantry)
Fort Gaines Guards (Company D, 9th Georgia Infantry)
Fort Valley Cavalry (Company —, 12th Georgia State Guards)
Franklin County Guards (Captain S. W. Kay's Company, Six Months' Local Defense Troops, Georgia)
Franklin County Reserves (Company C, Whitehead's Battalion, Local Defense Troops, Georgia)

Freeman Guards (Company G, 28th Georgia Infantry)
F. S. Slaters (Company —, —. Georgia —)
Fulton Dragoons (Company G, Cobb's Legion, Georgia Volunteers)
Gainesville Light Infantry (Company A, 11th Georgia Infantry)
Gardner Volunteers (Company H, 22d Georgia Infantry)
Garrison Guards Battalion (1st Regiment, Georgia State Line)
Georgia Dragoons (Company G, 2d Georgia Cavalry)
Georgia Defenders (Captain F. S. Chapman's Independent Company, Georgia State Troops)
Georgia Coast Rifles (Company F, 1st Volunteers, Georgia Infantry)
Georgia Dragoons (Company E, 4th (Avery's) Georgia Cavalry)
Georgia Mounted Dragoons (Company I, 4th (Avery's) Georgia Cavalry)
Georgia Fire Company (Company E, Augusta Fire Battalion Local Defense Troops, Georgia)
Georgia Forresters (Company F, 29th Georgia Infantry)
Georgia Guards (Company F, 6th Georgia Guards)
Georgia Hussars (Company A, Captain J. F. Waring's Independent Georgia Company; assigned October 14, 1861 as Company E, 6th Virginia Cavalry; relieved and assigned as Company F, Jeff Davis Legion, December 7, 1861)
Georgia Hussars (Company B, Captain W. H. Wiltberger, Company D, 2d Battalion, Georgia Cavalry)
Georgia Light Artillery (Captain Horatio N. Hollifield's Company, State Troops)
Georgia Light Infantry (Company A, 31st Georgia Infantry)
Georgia Rangers (Company G, 10th Georgia Infantry)
Georgia Rangers (62d Georgia Cavalry)
Georgia Regulars (See Hamilton Battery)
Georgia Troopers (Company C, 9th Georgia Cavalry)
Georgia Troopers (Company H, 9th Georgia Cavalry)
Georgia Volunteers (Company H, 2d Georgia Infantry)
German Volunteers (Company I, 1st Georgia Volunteers)
Gibson Guards (Company A, 48th Georgia Infantry)
Gilmer Battalion (Local Defense Troops, Georgia)
Gilmer Blues (Company K, 6th Georgia Infantry)
Gilmer Guards (Captain D. M. West's Company, Gilmer Battalion, Local Defense Troops, Georgia)
Gilmer Light Guards (Company B, Smith's Legion, Georgia Volunteers; afterward Company A, 65th Georgia Infantry)
Gilmer Rifles (Captain John E. Mitchell's Company, Jackson's Regiment, Georgia Volunteers)
Gilmer Volunteers (Company P, 60th Georgia Infantry)
Glascock Rangers (Captain R. Walden's Company, Stephens' Battalion, Local Defense Troops, Georgia)

Glover Guards (Company G, 4th Georgia Infantry)
Glynn Guards (Company A, 26th Georgia Infantry)
Glynn Guards (Company B, 4th (Clinch's) Georgia Cavalry)
Goshen Blues (Company H, 38th Georgia Infantry)
Governor's Guard (Company E, 3d Georgia Infantry)
Governor's Horse Guards (Company A, Cavalry Battalion, Phillips' Legion, Georgia)
Grant Factory Guards (Captain J. J. Grant's Company, Thompson's Battalion, Local Defense Troops, Georgia)
Gresham Rifles (Company, A, 45th Georgia Infantry)
Griffin Light Artillery (Captain O. C. Gibson's Company, Georgia Artillery)
Griffin Light Guards (Company B, 5th Georgia Infantry)
Grubb's Hussars (Company F, Cavalry Battalion, Cobb's Legion, Georgia)
Gwinnett Artillery (Company D, 9th Battalion, Georgia Artillery)
Gwinnett Cavalry (No. 1) (Company C, 10th Georgia State Guards)
Gwinnett Cavalry (No. 2) (Company H, 10th Georgia State Guards)
Gwinnett Greys (Company B, 8th Georgia State Guards)
Gwinnett Guards (Company C, 8th Georgia State Guards)
Habersham Defenders (Company D, Whitehead's Battalion, Local Defense Troops, Georgia)
Had's Partisan Rangers (Unattached Company —)
Hall Chattahoochee Cavalry (Company B. Blue Ridge Tiger Regiment, 4th Georgia State Guards)
Hall County Cavalry (Company A, Blue Ridge Tiger Regiment, 4th Georgia State Guards)
Hall Troopers (Company I, Blue Ridge Tiger Regiment, 4th Georgia State Guards)
Hall Volunteers (Company D, 55th Georgia Infantry)
Hamilton Battery (Also called Georgia Regulars, originally Company A, 1st Georgia Regulars; afterwards Independent Company, Georgia Artillery)
Hamilton Rangers (Company K, 48th Georgia Infantry)
Haralson Brown Guards (Company A, 35th Georgia Infantry)
Haralson Cavalry (Company E, McDonald's Battalion, Local Defense Troops, Georgia)
Hardee Rifles (Company H, 5th Georgia Infantry)
Hardee Rifles (Captain John L. Hardee's Company, Local Defense Troops, Georgia)
Hardwlck Mounted Rifles (Company H, 7th Georgia Cavalry)
Hargett Infantry (Company F, 5th Georgia State Guards)
Harris Dragoons (Company F, 12th Georgia State Guards)
Harris Guards (Company —, Georgia —)
Harrison Volunteers (Company G, 51st Georgia Volunteers)
Hartwell Infantry (Company C, 16th Georgia Infantry)

Hawkinsville Rangers (Company B, 19th Battalion, Georgia Cavalry)
Heard Independent Cavalry (Company E, 10th Georgia State Guards)
Henry County Cavalry (Company B, 10th Georgia State Guards)
Henry County Dragoons (Company F, 10th Georgia State Guards)
Henry Guards (Company G, 19th Georgia Infantry)
Henry Infantry (Company K, 8th Georgia State Guards)
Henry Light Infantry (Company B, 25th Georgia Infantry)
High Shoals Defenders (Captain A. J. Medlin's Company, Six Months' Local Defense Troops, Georgia)
Highland Rangers (Company G, 1st Georgia Cavalry)
Hillyer Rifles (Company C, 9th Georgia Infantry)
Holloway Greys (Captain A. J. White's Company, Georgia —)
Home Guards (Company D, 3d Georgia Infantry)
Homer Cavalry (Company F, Blue Ridge Tiger Regiment, 4th Georgia State Guards)
Homer Troopers (Company A, 30th Battalion, Georgia Cavalry)
Hood's Cavalry (Company D, 29th Battalion, Georgia Cavalry)
Hook and Ladder Guard (Company D, Atlanta Fire Battalion, Local Defense Troops, Georgia)
Hopkins Partisan Rangers (Company A, 24th Battalion, Georgia Cavalry)
Hopkins Partisan Rangers (Company C, 24th Battalion, Georgia Cavalry)
Houston Guard (Company A, 8th Battalion, Georgia State Guard)
Houston Volunteers (Company K, 11th Georgia Infantry)
Huguenin Rifles (Company D, 30th Georgia Infantry)
Hunter Guards (Company C, 30th Georgia Infantry)
Hunter Rifles (Company —, 4th Georgia Infantry)
Hurt Light Artillery (Lieutenant Joseph A. Alexander's Company, Georgia Artillery)
Hunchins Guard (Captain — Thomas's Company, Georgia Volunteers)
Independent Blues (Company D, 10th Georgia Infantry)
Independent Georgia Volunteers (Captain G. W. Lee's Company, Georgia Vounteers)
Independent Volunteers (Lieutenant James A. Damour's Company, Georgia Volunteers)
Independent Volunteers (Company A, 1st Confederate Georgia)
Independent Volunteers (Company E, 9th Battalion, Georgia State Guard)
Invincibles (Captain — Holmes' Company, Georgia Volunteers)
Irish Jasper Greens (Company A, 1st Volunteers, Georgia)
Irish Volunteer Guards (Company —, 8th Georgia Infantry, 1st Volunteers Georgia).
Irish Volunteers (Company A, Company D, 1st Georgia Volunteers)
Irish Volunteers Co. B (Company E, 1st Volunteers, Georgia)
Irwin Guard (Company A, 9th Georgia Infantry)

Irwin Artillery (Originally Company A, 9th Georgia Infantry; afterward Company C, Sumter 11th Battalion, Georgia Artillery)
Irwin Invincibles (Company E. 25th Georgia Infantry)
Irwin Volunteers (20th Georgia Infantry)
Irwin Volunteers (Company F, 49th Georgia Infantry)
Ivey Guards (Company G, 20th Georgia Infantry)
Ivey Guard (Company B, 5th Georgia State Guard)
Jack Brown's (Company H. 59th Georgia Infantry)
Jackson Artillery (Captain George A. Dure's Company, Georgia Artillery)
Jackson Avengers (Captain — Bradford's Company, Georgia, —)
Jackson Avengers (Company G, 55th Georgia Infantry)
Jackson Blues (Company B, 2d Georgia Infantry)
Jackson Cavalry (Company K, Blue Ridge Tiger Regiment, 4th Georgia State Guards)
Jackson Guards (Company B, 59th Georgia Infantry)
Jackson Mounted Guards (Company I, 9th Georgia State Guards)
Jasper Maxey Infantry (Company C, 6th Georgia State Guard)
Jeff's Cavalry (Captain H. G. Wright's Company, Local Defense Troops, Georgia)
Jefferson Guards (Company C. 20th Georgia Infantry)
Jefferson Volunteers (Company E, 48th Georgia Infantry)
Jennings Rangers (Company C, 20th Battalion, Georgia Cavalry)
Joe Brown Guard (Captain A. J. Smith's Company, Wilson's Battalion. Local Defense Troops, Georgia)
Joe Brown Rifles (Company G, Blue Ridge Tiger Regiment, 4th Georgia State Guards)
Joe Brown's, The (Company —, 2d Georgia —)
Joe Brown's Guards (Company F, 9th Georgia State Guards)
Joe Brown's Pets (Company C, 2d Georgia State Troops)
Johnson Guards (Company B, Cavalry Battalion, Phillips' Legion, Georgia Volunteers)
Jones Hussars (Captain J. J. Jones' Company, Six Months' Local Defense Troops, Georgia)
Jones State Guards (Company H, 6th Georgia State Guards)
Jones Volunteers (Company B, 12th Georgia Infantry)
Jo Thompson Artillery (Originally Company M, 38th Georgia Infantry; afterward Captain L. J. Parr's, afterward C. R. Hanleiter's Company, Georgia Artillery)
Kennesaw Guards (Company A, 7th Georgia State Guards)
LaFayette Volunteers (Company G, 9th Georgia Infantry)
LaGrange Light Guards (Company B, 4th Georgia Infantry)

Lamar Mounted Rifles (Also called Mounted Rifles, Company H, 5th Georgia Cavalry)
Lamar Rangers (Also called Mounted Rifles, Company H, 5th Georgia Cavalry)
Lamar Infantry (Company A, 54th Georgia Infantry)
Laurens Volunteers (Company G, 49th Georgia Infantry)
Lawrenceville Infantry (Company E, 8th Georgia State Guards)
Laurens Reserves (Captain R. A. Stanley's Company, Carswell's Battalion, Local Defense Troops, Georgia)
Lee Cavalry (Captain J. H. Allen's Cavalry, Six Months Local Defense Troops, Georgia)
Lee Guards (Company B, 51st Georgia Infantry)
Lee Riflemen (Company F, Whitehead's Battalion, Local Defense Troops, Georgia)
Lee Rifles (See Augusta Lee Rifles).
Lee Volunteers (Company B, 11th Georgia Infantry)
Lee Rangers (Company E, Provost Battalion, Local Defense Troops, Georgia)
Lee's Volunteers (Company D, 1st Battalion, Georgia Infantry)
Lester Volunteers (Company E, 14th Georgia Infantry)
Letcher Guards (Company B, 10th Georgia Infantry)
Lewis and Phillips Guards (Company C, 3d Battalion, Georgia Infantry)
Leyden Artillery (Company A, 9th Battalion, Georgia Artillery)
Liberty Company (Company A, Whitehead's Battalion, Local Defense Troops, Georgia)
Liberty Dragoons (Company B, 20th Battalion, Georgia Cavalry)
Liberty Mounted Dragoons (Company B, 20th Battalion, Georgia Cavalry)
Liberty Guards (Company D, 5th Georgia Cavalry)
Liberty Independent Troop (Company G, 5th Georgia Cavalry)
Liberty Mounted Rangers (See Liberty Dragoons)
Liberty Volunteers (Company H, afterward E, 25th Georgia Infantry)
Line Guards (Company D, Stephens' Battalion, Local Defense Troops, Georgia)
Lipscomb Volunteers (Company H, 9th Georgia State Guards)
Lochrane Guards (Company F, Infantry Battalion, Phillips' Legion, Georgia)
Lockett Volunteers (Company K, 59th Georgia Infantry)
Lowndes Mounted Infantry (Company B, 11th Georgia State Guards)
Lowndes Volunteers (Company I, 12th Georgia Infantry)
Lula Fire Company No. 3 (Company C, Atlanta Fire Battalion, Local Defense Troops, Georgia)
Lula Videttes (Company F, Atlanta Fire Battalion, Local Defense Troops, Georgia)
Lumpkin Cavalry (Captain B. H. Corbin's Company, Six Months Local Defense Troops, Georgia)

Lumpkin Guards (Company E, 30th Battalion, Georgia State Troops)
McCulloch Rifles (Company L, afterward D, 38th Georgia Infantry)
McDonald Battalion (— Battalion, Georgia State Guards)
McIntosh Cavalry (Company K, 5th Georgia Cavalry)
McIntosh County Guards (Company M, 26th Georgia Infantry)
McIntosh Guards (Company M, 26th Georgia Infantry)
McIntosh Guards (Captain — McIntosh's Company, Georgia —)
McIntosh Volunteers (Captain J. W. Boggs' Company, Georgia)
McLeod Artillery (originally Company C, 38th Georgia Infantry —Wright's Legion)
McLeod Volunteers (Company H, 48th Georgia Infantry)
Macon Battalion (Battalion Local Defense Troops, Georgia)
Macon County Volunteers (Company I, 4th Georgia Infantry)
Macon Guards (Company —, 2d Georgia Infantry)
Macon Guards (Company C, 8th Georgia Infantry)
Macon Provost Guard (Company —, — Georgia —)
Macon Volunteers (Company A, Company D, 2d Battalion, Georgia Infantry)
Macon Volunteers (Company B, Captain C. H. Freeman's Company, Macon Battalion, Local Defense Troops, Georgia).
Macon and Western Railroad Guards (Captain John S. Wise's Company, Macon Battalion, Local Defense Troops, Georgia)
Madison Greys (Company A, 16th Georgia Infantry)
Marietta Infantry (Company E, 7th Georgia State Guards)
Marion Guards (Company K, 12th Georgia Infantry)
Marion Infantry (Company H, 5th Georgia State Guards)
Marshallville Volunteers (Company —, 12th Georgia State Guards).
Maxwell Artillery (Also called Regular Light Battery, Captain J. A. Maxwell's Company, Georgia Artillery, originally Company D, 1st Georgia Regulars).
Mechanic Fire Company No. 2 (Company B, Atlanta Fire Battalion, Local Defense Troops, Georgia).
Mell Volunteers (Company D, Infantry Battalion, Cobb's Legion, Georgia Volunteers)
Mercer Artillery (Company K, 28th Battalion, Georgia Infantry)
Mercer Partisans (Company A, 24th Battalion, Georgia Cavalry)
Meriwether Volunteers (Company —, 13th Georgia Infantry)
Milledge Artillery (Captain John Milledge's (Jr.) Company, Georgia Artillery)
Milledgeville Guards (Captain Wm. Caraker's Company, Six Months Local Defense Troops, Georgia)
Millen Rifles (Company E, 8th Georgia Infantry)
Millen's Partisan Rangers (20th Battalion, Georgia Cavalry)
Miller Guard (Company D, 51st Georgia Infantry)
Miller Rangers (Company C, 21st Battalion, Georgia Cavalry)

Milton Cavalry (Company B, Cavalry Battalion, Cherokee Legion, Georgia Volunteers)
Milton Guards (Company B, 38th Georgia Infantry)
Mitchell Guards (Company C, 31st Georgia Infantry)
Mitchell Independents (Company F, 6th Georgia Infantry)
Mitchell Van-Guard (Company C, 51st Georgia Infantry)
Mitchell Volunteer Guards (Company A, 47th Georgia Infantry)
Monroe Crowders (Company D, 31st Georgia Infantry)
Monroe Infantry (Company D, 8th Georgia State Guards)
Montgomery Artillery (14th Battalion, Georgia Artillery)
Montgomery Guards (Guilmartin's Company, 1st Volunteers, Georgia, afterward Company E, 22d Battalion, Georgia Siege Artillery)
Montgomery Sharpshooters (Company E, 61st Georgia Infantry)
Montgomery Volunteers (Company —, Carswell's Battalion, Local Defense Troops, Georgia)
Moughon Infantry (Company D, 66th Georgia Infantry)
Moultrie Cavalry (Company C, 11th Georgia State Guards)
Mountain Dragoons (Company A, 23d Battalion, Georgia Infantry)
Mountain Rangers (Company E, 21st Georgia Infantry)
Mountain Tigers (Company H, 31st Georgia Infantry)
Mountaineer Riflemen (Company I, 48th Georgia Infantry)
Mountaineers (Company D, 14th Battalion, Georgia Artillery)
Mounted Infantry (Company B, 9th Battalion, Georgia State Guards)
Mounted Infantry (Captain J. J. Jones' Company, Six Months Local Defense Troops, Georgia)
Mounted Rangers (Lieutenant J. H. Sykes' Company, Georgia Cavalry)
Muckalee Guards (Company A, 12th Georgia Infantry)
Mumford Avengers (Company —, 49th Georgia Infantry)
Murphy Guards (Company A, 12th Georgia Infantry)
Murray Cavalry (Captain W. C. Asher's Independent Company, Georgia Cavalry)
Murray Rifles (Company —, Georgia —)
Muscogee Cavalry (Company —, 12th Georgia State Guards)
Muscogee Confederates (Company B, 31st Georgia Infantry)
Muscogee Factory Guards (Company —, Thompson's Battalion, Georgia Volunteers)
Muscogee Guards (Captain A. B. Thornton's Company, Six Months Local Defense Troops, Georgia)
Muscogee Light Infantry (Company B, 20th Georgia Infantry)
Muscogee Rifles (Company E, 12th Georgia Infantry)
Muscogee Rifles (Company —, — Georgia —)
Nelson Rangers (T. M. Nelson's Independent Company, Georgia Cavalry, General S. D. Lee's Escort)

Newnan Artillery (Company A, (Hanvey's Battery) 12th Battalion, Georgia Artillery)
Newnan Guards (Company A, 1st Georgia Volunteers)
Newnan Rangers (42d Georgia Infantry)
Ochlochnee Light Infantry (Company B, 29th Georgia Infantry)
Ocmulgee Rangers (Company A, 19th Battalion, Georgia Cavalry; afterward Company F, 10th Confederate Cavalry).
Oconee Guards (Company K, 9th Georgia State Guards)
Oconee Scouts (Capt. J. S. Joyner's Company, Georgia Volunteers)
Oconee Volunteers (Captain — Thompson's Company, Georgia Volunteers)
Ogeechee Minute Men (Captain D. W. Garrison's Company, Six Months Local Defense Troops, Georgia)
Ogeechee Rifles (Company K, afterward D. 25th Georgia Infantry)
Oglethorpe Artillery (Company —, 8th Georgia Volunteers)
Oglethorpe Blues (Company —,— Georgia —)
Oglethorpe Guards (Company D, 1st Georgia Volunteers)
Oglethorpe Infantry (Company D, 1st Volunteers, Georgia)
Oglethorpe Light Artillery (Company A, 63d Georgia Infantry)
Oglethorpe Light Infantry (Company H, 1st Volunteers, Georgia)
Oglethorpe Light Infantry (Company B, 8th Georgia Infantry)
Oglethorpe Rifles (Company K, 8th Georgia Infantry)
Oglethorpe Siege Artillery Battalion (Independent Battalion, Georgia Artillery, Companies A and B—Company A became Company C (formerly Savannah Artillery) and Company B became Company D, 22d Battalion, Georgia Siege Artillery)
O. K. Rifles (Company —, 13th Georgia Infantry)
Okefenokee Rifles (Company F, afterward G, 26th Georgia Infantry)
One Company (Company G, Atlanta Fire Battalion, Local Defense Troops Georgia)
Ordnance Guard (Local Defense Georgia Volunteers, Macon, Georgia).
Palmetto Guards (Company C, 19th Georgia Infantry)
Panola Guards (Company G, 9th Georgia Cavalry)
Panola Guards (Rifles) (Company H, 13th Georgia Infantry)
Paulding Infantry (Company K, Infantry Battalion, Floyd Legion, Georgia State Guards)
Paulding Raid Repellers (Company A, McDonald's Battalion, Local Defense Troops Georgia)
Paulding Volunteers (Company C, 7th Georgia Infantry)
Pauline Rifles (Captain W. H. Barteley's Company, 5th Georgian State Troops)
Perry Cavalry (Company —, 12th Georgia State Guards)
Phillips Battalion (Georgia State Guards)
Phillips Legion (Georgia Volunteers)

Phoenix Battalion (Company C, 13th Battalion, Georgia Volunteers)
Phoenix Riflemen (Company —, 1st Volunteers, Georgia; afterward Company B, 63d Georgia Infantry)
Pickens Cavalry (Company D, McDonald's Battalion, Local Defense Troops, Georgia)
Pickens Raid Repellers (Company I, Cherokee Legion, Georgia Infantry)
Pierce Guards (Company I, 49th Georgia Infantry)
Pierce Mounted Volunteers (Also called Atlantic and Gulf Guards Cavalry Company attached to 26th Georgia Infantry)
Pike Infantry (Company E, 6th Georgia State Guards)
Pioneer Infantry (Company E, Augusta Fire Brigade, Local Defense Troops. Georgia)
Pirkle Rangers (Company —, Blue Ridge Tiger Regiment, 4th Georgia State Guards)
Piscola Volunteers (Company I, 26th Georgia Infantry)
Pochitla Guards (Company E, 51st.Georgia Infantry)
Polk Mounted Infantry (Company H, Cavalry Battalion, Floyd Legion, Georgia State Guards)
Polk Volunteers (Company G, Infantry Battalion, Floyd Legion, Georgia State Guards)
Pond Spring Company—Cavalry—(Company E, Culberson's Battalion. Local Defense Troops, Georgia)
Poythree Volunteers (Company E, Infantry Battalion, Cobb's Legion, Georgia Volunteers).
Provost Battalion (Battalion at Macon, Georgia)
Provost Guard (Battalion at Atlanta, Georgia)
Pulaski Artillery (Company K, 10th Georgia Infantry; afterward attached as Company L or K to 1st Virginia Artillery)
Pulaski Guards (Company K, 10th Georgia Infantry; afterward attached as Company L or K to 1st Virginia Artillery)
Pulaski Blues, (Company F, 31st Georgia Infantry)
Pulaski Cavalry (Company —, Carswell's Battalion, Local Defense Troops, Georgia)
Pulaski Greys (Company K, 49th Georgia Infantry)
Pulaski Guard (Captain H. Williams' Company, Georgia Infantry)
Pulaski Volunteers (Company G, 8th Georgia Infantry)
Putnam Infantry (Company —, Georgia Infantry)
Putnam Light Infantry (Company G, 12th Georgia Infantry)
Quitman Greys (Company —, 11th Georgia Infantry)
Quitman Guards (Company K, 1st Georgia Volunteers)
Quitman Guards (Company K, 53rd Georgia Infantry)
Railroad Guards (Company —, Thompson's Battalion, Local Defense Troops, Georgia)

Railroad Guards (Captain J. J. Matthews' Company, Georgia Volunteers)
Rains Guards (Company D, Rains' Regiment, Local Defense Troops, Augusta (?), Georgia)
Ramsey Volunteers (Company K, 16th Georgia Infantry)
Randolph Cavalry (Company A, 2d Georgia Cavalry)
Randolph Rangers (Company B, 24th Battalion, Georgia Cavalry)
Randolph Rangers (Company G, 51st Georgia Infantry)
Randolph Volunteers (Company —, 13th Georgia Infantry)
Rattlesnake Rangers (Company C, 19th Battalion, Georgia Cavalry)
Rebel Rangers (Company D, 2d Georgia State Guards)
Reese Guards (Company B, 9th Georgia State Guards)
Reids' Guards (Company C, 39th Battalion, Georgia State Troops)
Republican Blues (Originally a Battalion of Georgia Militia; afterward Companies B and C 1st Volunteers, Georgia Infantry)
Reserve Chatham Artillery (Georgia Artillery)
Richmond Dragoons (Company K, Cavalry Battalion, Cobb's Legion, Georgia Volunteers)
Richmond Hussars (Company A, Cavalry Battalion, Cobb's Legion, afterward 9th Georgia Cavalry)
Richmond Light Infantry (Company D, Augusta Fire Battalion, Local Defense Troops, Georgia)
Rlgdon Guards (Captain A. J. Smith's Company, Local Defense Troops, Georgia)
Ringgold Rangers (Company C, 13th Georgia Infantry)
Ringgold Guard (Georgia)
Ringgold Rangers (Captain A. C. Bradshaw's Company (Independent) Georgia Cavalry)
Ringgold Volunteers (Company B, 1st Battalion, Georgia Infantry)
Rome Cavalry (Company C, Cavalry Battalion, Floyd Legion. Georgia State Guards)
Rome Guards (Company A, Infantry Battalion, Floyd Legion, Georgia State Guards)
Rome Light Guards (Company A, 8th Georgia Infantry)
Roswell Battalion (Cavalry) Local Defense Troops, Georgia)
Roswell Troopers (Company —, Cavalry Battalion, Cobb's Legion, Georgia Volunteers), afterward Company E, 9th Georgia Cavalry)
Rough and Ready Boys (Captain —, Richards' Company, Georgia Volunteers)
Rough aad Ready Boys (Captain —, McRae's Company, Georgia Volunteers)
Rough and Ready Volunteers (Company G, 7th Georgia State Guards)
Rowan Partisan Rangers (Company K, 6th Georgia Cavalry)
Rutland Guards (Company B, 27th Georgia Infantry)
Rutledge Sharpshooters (Company —, Georgia)

Sallacoa Silver Greys (Company F, Infantry Battalion, Cherokee Legion, Georgia Volunteers)
Sallie Twiggs Regiment (16th Georgia Infantry)
Sardis Volunteers (Company E, 21st Georgia Artillery)
Satilla Rangers (Company A, 50th Georgia Infantry)
Savannah Artillery (Captain J. B. Gallie's Company Georgia Artillery, originally attached to 1st Volunteers, Georgia Infantry)
Savannah Cadets (Company —, Georgia —)
Savannah City Light Guard (Also called City Light Guard, Company D, 1st Volunteers, Georgia Infantry)
Savannah Guards (18th Battalion Georgia Infantry)
Savannah Volunteers (18th Battalion, Georgia Infantry)
Savannah Volunteer Guards (18th Battalion, Georgia Infantry)
Savannah Volunteer Guards (A company of boys (Captain W. G. Charlton's Company, Georgia Volunteers)
Savannah River Guards (Company K, — Georgia)
Schley Cavalry (Company D, 29th Battalion, Georgia Cavalry)
Schley Riflemen (Company A, 22d Georgia Infantry)
Schley Volunteers (Company B, 17th Georgia Infantry)
Scott Infantry (Company B, 64th Georgia Infantry)
Screven Cavalry (Company —, Wright's Battalion, Local Defense Troops, Georgia)
Screven Guards (Company D, 45th Georgia Infantry)
Screven Troop (Company B, 2d Battalion, Georgia Cavalry)
Seaboard Guards (Company C, 26th Georgia Infantry)
Second Independent Battalion Infantry (Georgia Volunteers)
Semmes Guard (Company C, 2d Georgia Infantry)
"Seventeenth" Patriots (Company K, 29th Georgia Infantry)
Shiloh Troop (Company K, 4th (Clinch's) Georgia Cavalry)
Sidney Johnstons (Company G, 59th Georgia Infantry)
Silver Greys (afterward called Bibb Greys (Company A, Rains' Regiment, Local Defense Troops, Georgia)
Slappey Guards (Company G, 48th Georgia Infantry)
Slocomb Volunteers (Company B, Whitehead's Battalion, Local Defense Troops, Georgia)
Sons of Dixie (Company G, 20th Georgia Infantry)
Southern Guards (Company B, 1st Georgia Volunteers)
Southern Guards (Company G) (Company I, 20th Georgia Infantry)
Southern Rifles (Company A, 4th Georgia Infantry)
Southern Rights Battery (Company A, 14th Battalion, Georgia Artillery)
Southern Rights Guards (Company C, 1st Georgia Volunteers)
Southern Rights Volunteers (Company A, 25th Georgia Infantry)

Southwestern Railroad Guards (Captain J. M. Walden's Company, Macon Battalion, Local Defense Troops, Georgia)
Southwestern Railroad Infantry (Captain C. D. Wall's Company, Macon Battalion, Local Defense Troops, Georgia)
Spalding Greys (Company B, 2d Independent Battalion, Georgia Infantry)
Spalding Infantry (Company I, 6th Georgia State Guards)
Spalding Volunteers (Company K, 6th Georgia State Guards)
Stark Guards (Company F, 61st Georgia Infantry)
Stark Volunteers (Company I, 13th Georgia Infantry)
State Armory Guards (Captain J. W. Green's Company, Six Months Local Defense Troops, Georgia)
State Rights Guards (Company E, 49th Georgia Infantry)
Stephens Battalion (Battalion Georgia State Guards)
Stephens Home Guard (Company D, 15th Georgia Infantry)
Stephens Light Artillery (Georgia Artillery; prior to November 1863, 3d Maryland Battery)
Stephens Light Guard (Company I, 8th Georgia Infantry)
Stephens Rifles (Company C, 9th Georgia Cavalry)
Stephens Volunteers (Company G, 29th Georgia Infantry)
Stewart Greys (Company K, 2d Georgia Infantry)
Stewart Infantry (Company —, Yarborough's Battalion, Local Defense Troops, Georgia).
Stewart Infantry (Company I, 21st Georgia Infantry)
Stone Mountain Guards (Company H, 8th Georgia State Guards)
Stonewall Cavalry (Company —, 12th Georgia State Guards)
Stonewall Guards (Company D, 6th Georgia State Guards)
Stonewall Hussars Lieutenant J. D. Harrell's Company, Georgia Volunteers)
Stonewall Volunteers (Company A, 5th Georgia State Guards)
Sulphur Spring Guard (Company B, 2d Georgia State Guard)
Sumter Battalion (11th Battalion Georgia Artillery)
Sumter Cavalry (Company —, 12th Georgia State Guards)
Sumter Flying Artillery (Captain A. S. Cutts' Company, Georgia Artillery; afterward Company A, 11th Battalion Georgia Artillery)
Sumter Light Guards (Company K, 4th Georgia Infantry)
Swamp Rangers (Company D, 19th Battalion, Georgia Cavalry)
Sydney Brown Infantry (Captain —, Arnold's Company Georgia Volunteers)
Talbot Guards (Company E, 9th Georgia Infantry)
Talbot Infantry (Company F, 5th Georgia State Guards)
Talbot Troopers (Company —, 12th Georgia State Guards)
Taliaferro Volunteers (Company D, 49th Georgia Infantry)
Tattnall Invincibles (Company G, 47th Georgia Infantry)
Tattnall Rangers (Company B, 61st Georgia Infantry)
Tattnall Guards (Company G, 1st Volunteers, Georgia Infantry)

Taylor Cavalry (Company —, 12th Georgia State Guards)
Taylor Infantry (Company K, 5th Georgia State Guards)
Telfair Irish Greys (Company A, 25th Georgia Infantry)
Telfair Volunteers (Company B, 48th Georgia Infantry)
Telfair Volunteers (Company H, 20th Georgia Infantry)
Terrell Infantry (Company F, 51st Georgia Infantry)
Terrell Light Artillery (Captain E. G. Dawson's Company, Georgia Artillery)
Thomas Cavalry (Company A, 11th Georgia State Guards)
Thomas County Rangers (Company E, 50th Georgia Infantry)
Thomas County Volunteers (Company H, 29th Georgia Infantry)
Thomas Legion (Georgia Volunteers)
Thomas Reserves (Captain A. H. Hamell's (Hahsell's) Company, Georgia Volunteers)
Thomasville Guards (Company A, 29th Georgia Infantry)
Thompson Guard, 7th Battalion Georgia)
Thompson Guards (Company F, 10th Georgia Infantry)
Thompson Guards (Company —, 13th Georgia —)
Thompson Guards (Company I, 61st Georgia Infantry)
Thompson Rangers (Company D, 2d Georgia Infantry)
Tilton Volunteers (Company B, 1st Georgia State Guards)
Toccoa Infantry (Company G, Whitehead's Battalion, Local Defense Troops, Georgia)
Tom Cobb Infantry (Company E, 38th Georgia Infantry)
Toombs Guards (Company I, 9th Georgia Infantry)
Toombs Rangers (Company D, 20th Georgia Infantry)
Toombs Rangers (Company C, 21st Georgia Infantry)
Toombs Volunteers (Company F, 4th Georgia Infantry)
Town Rangers (Company A, Cavalry Battalion, Smith's Legion, Georgia Volunteers)
Troup Artillery (Originally attached to 2d Georgia Infantry, afterward Company A, Cobb's Legion, afterward Captain M. Stanley's Independent Company Georgia Artillery)
Tugalo Rangers (Company D, 30th Battalion, Georgia Cavalry)
Turner Guards (Company I, 59th Georgia Infantry)
Twiggs Cavalry (Company —, Carswell's Battalion, Local Defense Troops, Georgia)
Twiggs Guards (Company I, 6th Georgia Infantry)
Twiggs Volunteers (Company C, 4th Georgia Infantry)
Valdosta Guards (Company D, 50th Georgia Infantry)
Valley Rangers (Company D, — Georgia —)
Vason Guards (Captain P. Robinson's Company, Georgia Volunteers)
Vigilant Infantry (Company A, Augusta Fire Brigade, Local Defense Troops, Georgia)

Walker Cavalry (Company A, Culberson's Battalion, Local Defense Troops, Georgia)
Walker Cavalry (Company B, Culberson's Battalion, Local Defense Troops, Georgia)
Walker Cavalry (Company C, Culberson's Battalion, Local Defense Troops, Georgia)
Walker Independents (Company C, 60th Georgia Infantry)
Walker Light Infantry (Company I, 1st Georgia Volunteers)
Walker Rifles (Company E, 55th Georgia Infantry)
Walton Guards (Company E, 9th Georgia State Guards)
Walton Infantry (Company H, 11th Georgia Infantry)
Walton Rangers (Company —, 10th Georgia State Guards)
War Department Guards (Company A, 3d Battalion. Local Defense Troops, Georgia)
Ward Volunteers (Company C, 9th Georgia State Guards)
Ware Guards (Company D, 26th Georgia Infantry)
Ware Volunteers (Company B, 50th Georgia Infantry)
Ware Volunteers (Company —, 11th Georgia State Guards)
Warren Akin Guards (Company E, 64th Georgia Infantry)
Warren Defenders (Company —, Wilson's Battalion, Local Defense Troops, Georgia)
Warren Infantry (Company B, 48th Georgia Infantry)
Warsaw Rifles (Company C, 25th Georgia Infantry)
Washington Artillery (Assigned as Company F to 1st Independent Battalion, afterward Company F, 1st Confederate Volunteers, 36th Georgia Infantry; afterward Burtwell's and Pritchard's Batteries)
Washington County Company (Company E, 1st Georgia Volunteers)
Washington Guards (Company C, 49th Georgia Infantry)
Washington Light Infantry (Company B, Augusta Fire Battalion, Local Defense Troops, Georgia)
Washington Rifles (Company B, 32d Georgia Infantry)
Washington Rifles (Company E, 1st Georgia Volunteers)
Washington volunteers (Company K, 1st Volunteers, Georgia Infantry)
Wayne Cavalry Guards (Company Six Months Local Defense Troops, Georgia)
Wayne Guards (Company G, 6th Georgia State Guards)
Wayne & Mercer Rangers (Company A, 24th Battalion, Georgia Cavalry)
Wayne Rangers (Company A, 4th (Clinch's Georgia Cavalry)
Wayne Rangers (Company A, 24th Battalion, Georgia Cavalry)
Webster Invincibles (46th Georgia Infantry)
Webster Rifles (Company A, 17th Georgia Infantry)
West Infantry (Company E, Whitehead's Battalion, Local Defense Troops, Georgia)

West Point Guards (Company D, 4th Georgia Infantry)
Western & Atlantic Guards (Captain — Hull's Company, Georgia Infantry)
White Home Guards (Company G, 8th Georgia State Guards).
Whitesvllle Guards (Company E, 20th Georgia Infantry)
Whitfield Volunteers (Company D, 60th Georgia Infantry)
Whittle Guards (Company D, 10th Battalion, Georgia Infantry)
Wilcox Cavalry Greys (Company —, Carswell's Battalion, Local Defense Troops, Georgia)
Wilcox Rifles (Company H, 10th Georgia Infantry)
Wilkerson Rifles (Company F, 3d Georgia Infantry)
Wilkinson Invincibles (Company A, 49th Georgia Infantry)
Wilkinson Volunteers (Company O, Carswell's Battalion, Local Defense Troops, Georgia)
Wilkinson Volunteers (Company A, 6th Georgia State Guards)
Williams Volunteers (Company C, 32d Georgia Infantry)
Wilson Tigers (Company I, 48th Georgia Infantry)
Wiregrass Boys (Company A, 20th Battalion, Georgia Cavalry)
Wiregrass Minutemen (Company C, 26th Georgia Infantry)
Wiregrass Rifle Company (Company F, 26th Georgia Infantry)
Worth Infantry (Company F, 59th Georgia Infantry)
Worth Reserves (Company Six Months Local Defense Troops, Georgia)
Wright Infantry (Company H, 2d Georgia Infantry)
Wright's Legion (38th Georgia Infantry)
Yancey Invincibles (Company H, 21st Georgia Infantry)
Young Guards (Company A, 3d Georgia Infantry)
Zollicoffer Riflemen (Company C, 10th Battalion, Georgia Infantry)

The Author on YouTube

There are several extracts of lectures by the author on Civil War topics available on YouTube, including:

Sherman's March: Strategy and Results
(http://www.youtube.com/watch?v=gAcqx0rpWXY)

Sherman's March: The Fall of Savannah
(http://www.youtube.com/watch?v=Iykjb7vA3wI)

Overview of the Great Locomotive Chase
(http://www.youtube.com/watch?v=CSJ03W8mlMc)

Author singing *"Hold the Fort"*
(http://www.youtube.com/watch?v=5LzWtVXAYAE)

Civil War Quick Note: Clara Barton
(http://youtu.be/7Td0lu49hsw)

A Brief Look at Patrick Cleburne
(http://youtu.be/qagsf7uUgZo)

A Brief Look at "Bloody Bill" Anderson
(http://youtu.be/Y-vA6BKaOWA)

All of these can be viewed in high definition (720p).

The author is available for lectures in Georgia, Alabama, southern Tennessee and eastern Kansas. For details, see: http://www.rcjbooks.com/guest_speaker.

About the Author

Robert is President of the Kennesaw Historical Society, and is a member of the Executive Board of the Kennesaw Museum Foundation. He is also an at-large board member for the Civil War Round Table of Cobb County. He has written several books on Civil War and railroad themes, including:

- *A Guide to the Civil War in Georgia*
- *Battle of Allatoona Pass: The Forgotten Battle of Sherman's Atlanta Campaign, The*
- *Battle of Chickamauga: A Brief History, The*
- *Battle of Griswoldville: An Infantry Battle on Sherman's March to the Sea, The*
- *Bleeding Kansas: The Real Start of the Civil War*
- *Civil War Prison Camps: A Brief History*
- *Confederate Invasion of New Mexico, The*
- *Famous Songs of the Civil War*
- *Fifteen Most Critical Moments of the Civil War, The*
- *Images of America: Kennesaw*
- *McCook's Raid and the Battle of Brown's Mill*
- *Pennsylvania Railroad: An Illustrated Timeline, The*
- *Reading Railroad: An Illustrated Timeline, The*
- *Retracing the Route of Sherman's Atlanta Campaign (expanded edition)*
- *Retracing the Route of Sherman's Atlanta Campaign and March to the Sea*
- *Retracing the Route of Sherman's March to the Sea (expanded edition)*
- *Top 10 Reasons Why the Civil War Was Won in the West, The*
- *Ten Best – and Worst – Generals of the Civil War, The*
- *Top 20 Civil War Spies and Secret Agents, The*
- *Top 20 Railroad Songs of All Time, The*
- *Top 25 Most Influential Women of the Civil War, The*
- *W&A, the General, and the Andrews Raid: A Brief History, The*

Robert C. Jones is an ordained elder in the Presbyterian Church. He has written and taught numerous adult Sunday School courses. He is also the author of:

- *25 Most Influential Protestant Leaders in England, The*
- *25 Most Influential Protestant Leaders in the United States, The*

- *25 Most Important Events in the Post-Apostolic Christian Church, The*
- *25 Most Influential Books in the Post-Apostolic Christian Church, The*
- *25 Most Influential People in the Post-Apostolic Christian Church, The*
- *25 Most Influential Women in the Post-Apostolic Church, The*
- *25 People Who Most Influenced the Music of Christianity, The*
- *A Brief History of Protestantism in the United States*
- *A Brief History of the Sacraments: Baptism and Communion*
- *Crusades and the Inquisition: A Brief History, The*
- *Crusades: Christendom Fights Back, The*
- *Heaven and Hell: In the Bible, the Apocrypha and the Dead Sea Scrolls*
- *Meet the Apostles: Biblical and Legendary Accounts*
- *Monks and Monasteries: A Brief History*
- *Origins of the New Testament, The*
- *Between the Testaments: Pharisees, Sadducees and Essenes*
- *Revelation: Background and Commentary*
- *Top 25 Misconceptions About Christianity, The*

Robert has also written several books on "Old West" themes, including:

- *Death Valley Ghost Towns – As They Appear Today*
- *Ghost Towns of Southern Arizona and New Mexico*
- *Ghost Towns of the Mojave National Preserve*
- *Ghost Towns of Western Nevada*
- *Top 10 Gunslingers and Lawmen of the Old West, The*

In 2005, Robert co-authored a business-oriented book entitled *Working Virtually: The Challenges of Virtual Teams*.

In 2013, Robert authored a book on World War I, entitled *The Top 10 Innovations of World War I*.

Also in 2013, Robert published *The Leo Beuerman Story: As Told by his Family*.

http://www.rcjbooks.com/
jone442@bellsouth.net